AF251839

BY ROBERT KELLY

Armed Descent (1961)

Her Body Against Time (1963)

Round Dances (1964)

Enstasy (1964)

Lunes (1964)

Lectiones (1965)

Words in Service (1965)

Weeks (1966)

The Scorpions (1967)

Song XXIV (1967)

Devotions (1967)

Twenty Poems (1967)

Axon Dendron Tree (1967)

Crooked Bridge Love Society (1967)

A Joining (1967)

Alpha (1968)

Finding the Measure (1968)

Sonnets (1968)

Statement (1968)

Songs I-XXX (1968)

The Common Shore (1969)

A California Journal (1969)

Kali Yuga (1970)

Cities (1971)

In Time (1971)

Flesh Dream Book (1971)

Ralegh (1972)

The Pastorals (1972)

Reading Her Notes (1972)

The Tears of Edmund Burke (1973)

The Mill of Particulars (1973)

A Line of Sight (1974)

The Loom (1975)

Sixteen Odes (1976)

The Lady Of (1977)

The Convections (1978)

Wheres (1978)

The Book of Persephone (1978)

The Cruise of the Pnyx (1979)

Kill the Messenger Who Brings Bad News (1979)

Sentence (1980)

Spiritual Exercises (1981)

The Alchemist to Mercury (1981)

Mulberry Women (1982)

Under Words (1983)

Thor's Thrush (1984)

A Transparent Tree (1985)

The Scorpions (new edition, 1985)

Not This Island Music (1987)

Doctor of Silence (1988)

Oahu (1988)

Cat Scratch Fever (1990)

Ariadne (1991)

A Strange Market (1992)

Editor

A Controversy of Poets (1965)

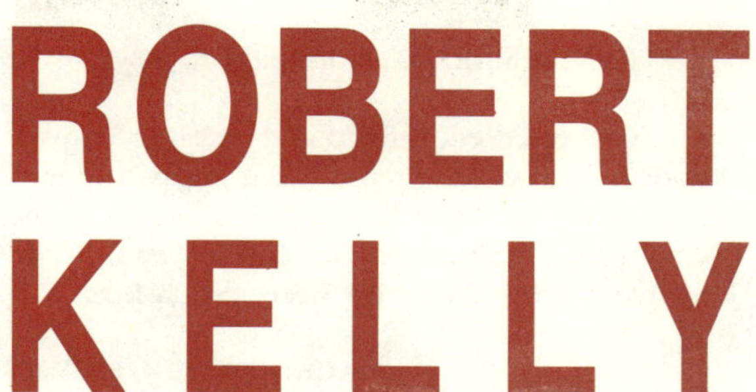

BLACK SPARROW PRESS

SANTA ROSA ■ 1992

ACKNOWLEDGEMENTS

The poems in this book were composed between 1986 and 1990. Most appear here for the first time in print, but a few have already been published in magazines: *Absinthe, Conjunctions, Hodos, Manuskripte, Mini, Notus, O-blek.* "A Flower for the New Year" appears in *The Best American Poetry 1991,* ed. Mark Strand (Scribners, 1991). "Fin de Siècle" appeared as the 1991 Christmas Broadside from the Poetry Collection of the Lockwood Memorial Library at SUNY Buffalo. "Air for English Horn" was printed by Paul Woodbine as a memorial card for Mary Moore Goodlett. "Avarice" was first published in *Dark Ages Clasp the Daisy Root.*

Unquell the Dawn Now is a homeophonic translation of Friedrich Hölderlin's great ode on the source of the Danube, *Am Quell der Donau.* It was published in the Austrian journal *Manuskripte,* Graz, along with Hölderlin's original; my version was furnished in turn with a profoundly gnostical translation into German by the poet Schuldt. The poem also appears in a *livre d'artiste* printed by Ilse Schreiber, a celebration of poems by and about Hölderlin.

In Titian Seen responds to paintings in the great collection shown at the National Gallery in the winter of 1990–91. The artist, in one of his last appearances in the census entries, gives his age as 103.

I am thankful for a research grant from Bard College that helped the preparation of this collection. And thanks are due Annie Boyd and Peg Cunningham for their various assistances.

I want especially to thank Charlotte Mandell for giving the manuscript its first reading, and for her clarity, patience and insight in helping me edit the final version.

Black Sparrow Press books are printed on acid-free paper.

LIBRARY OF CONGRESS CATALOGING-IN-PUBLICATION DATA

Kelly, Robert, 1935-
    A strange market / Robert Kelly.
      p.   cm.
    ISBN 0-87685-876-0 (cloth) : —ISBN 0-87685-875-2 (pbk.) :
  ISBN 0-87685-877-9 (cloth signed) :
    I. Title.
PS3521.E4322S77   1992
  811'.54—dc20   92-15230
                                                  CIP

*In the mountains there is a strange market
where you can trade the bewilderment of life
for unbounded happiness*

—from *The Life of Milarepa*

this book is for Mary Moore Goodlett
1950–1990

who shows me so much of the way.

TABLE OF CONTENTS

IN THE LIGHT

MIND THE GAP

AFTERDEATH

A STRANGE MARKET

IN THE LIGHT

IN THE LIGHT

Where did I see you? In the mistaken light
between competence and performance

in the protestant light I cherish
dusty scarlet, light of a high church modest candle,
sanctuary light, real presence,

in the protestant light of presence,
in the presence of light, light
is always adequate

in the light between desire and performance,
in the mistaken light between
the rule and the sentence, the bleak
light over Kaminstein's Hardware,
lost marriages, all our olive natures
ancient, goat-gnawed,
in the dawning light between
desire and the expression of desire,

in the episcopal light
that makes you take off your violet shirt
and still your skin shows that color,
morning light coming in off the snow

in the snow light between danger and desire,
for lust driveth out terror
in the urbane light of South Kensington
between a museum and what it shows,
between a replica and an original, a door,
light of a door, light of your areoles
purple in the fluted light of my mouth
kissing them tight, in the light
that rides inside us on our tongues our hands
in the interpenetrant light between
Shakertown and Harrodsburg, in mountain light,
in the light inside a glass of wine,
a wine I never drink, light of absence,
where is your mouth to me

in the light of absence I pray all distance
become our one same house, stone chimney
in the light of burning wood, light
between syntax and intention,
light between how you excite me
and what I answer,
crimson light of expectation, in the soft
light of commercial arrangements, in the moneyed
light of pleasant restaurants in snowy suburbs, with ferns,

in the lesbian light that touches every woman,
in the light that finds you, in the orange
light of dissidence, lambda light, the ruddy
light they serve in catholic churches, in glasses,
in Mary light, blue light, in the brown
light of leather, of lore,
yellow flowers of woad light,

in the light of books you give me
in the light of your love understanding me
in the light of my darkness receiving—

And on the other end of the pier,
the part called Night,
there is a light now everybody knows
though everybody goes there and that light
is in every body. The knowers know
and the be-ers are.
Here the waves are sharp,
rims etched against the lower sky,
light carved into light,
intaglio light showing through in cloud,
amber light of rainstorm, crimson
light just before sunset, sideways light,

mother light that nothing sees
mother light that all forgives
mother light that wounds, or wounded light
meat light, Greek light,
eye light is skin light, light
of the oldest languages you speak,
low-waisted light, light of a belt around your waist,
light of silver thread in silk,
light around the earth, zone light,
house of tragedy full of comic light,
my arm around you light what do you see,

tree light snow light everything
washed away by that ocean they call Night now
I call it nothing it doesn't
see me it forgives my caress,

virgin light, palpable, pure
as a flag, pure as an unknown word
in an unknown language spoken by your mouth,

speak it, pure as my sleep, pure light
and North Sea coast light, pure
light and California light, light
of every street I've ever known,
light of every house and every car's light,

pain light, light inside bones broken or whole,
cheap light of understood ideas,
bad light of getting what I want, fierce
light of wanting, dear light of unknown roads,
light of someone at the door.

WOOL

How could I forget the wool of my coat
or the rain on my lawn?
Love has carried nearer things away

and left men musing, strange on mountains,
looking over borders into sunlit prairies,
hearing indecipherable tongues.
This road,

this gentle desperate tiny road. This rod
whose magic spells make us cling together
tight and every other thing release.
And what we do now we have done before.

BRAHMS

to share with Mary Moore

Sexual differences unfold by dream
to know you and you a piece of Brahms
or carry in a host of satisfactions
grouped as "love" this wonderplace

and all the time skin just analyzes skin
justly bounce of Liebeslieder waltzes
laughing in red despite all the histories
how long it took this song to kiss you

the fact of land we didn't plan
under pine trees smell in winter balsam shiver
and time can chill them too together
are we born in the funeral *Ein deutsches*

Requiem 1857–68 is it death that tacits us together
if we did not die there'd be nothing to remember
a man who lives on mountains needs no music
and all you heard was what you sang

hill or hole a taste you member
in the long silences that pass for waking
sand the edges of it smooth and call it talking
and go to bed between the cat and the fugue

candle dinners us and then the green
becoming union shimmer of our food if only
mind relented to be any
then these improper particles an utter galaxy

made out of sound mind beyond mind
who listens to you talk me
as late as 1895 could still conduct
the ceremony knows your deepest mouth

say my dear how your fingers spine
of my piano undertaken bread of bed
and wine of milk sleep's undertow in northern lust
our exile a week only music's quarters sound

Brahms wouldn't go to to Cambridge would he
though we did to taste each other's traces
to hear rubaiyat fourfoldness of every actual thing
our nature is to be mind at last

movement's fugue all a-piece with going
together with you passionate civility
the energy the ceilings of Paradise acoustic
wooden coffered over the piano the

"wing" in German ferocious rubato pause
in intellect a dreamy southern sky
it is the last movement now those Cambridge bells
blue evenings out the Chesterton road

or far a dozen miles rise isle from marshlands
the magic octagon of Ely lifts a clue
against empty heaven a threat of sense
a strict notation for how each lover moves.

THALAMION

Come up the dry staircase
to the shadow bedroom very clean.
A window in it is full of trees
and a little writing desk nearby
holds mostly pens. Let him write you
again, you who have been spread
on so many sheets. Here
as everywhere it will be neat,
intense, pleasurable,
forgettable. This will not last.
That is the beauty of every it.

Let him put a crown on you then,
not on your head but on your hips.
Let him work it up your legs
and lodge it tight against your flesh.
This is the queen that rules him,
your between. Just where the diamond
gazes bluest at itself in such delight
there is the chief ornament of it and thee,
the middle of the middle, the little
room. Where he anoints you
with an oil you press from him.

SINAI

From the quartz heater a column
of red-orange heat arrives
marching towards me in the dingy room.

Here I live alone
in the region of the summer snow
blue shadows and sluggish
wasps my messengers.

Tell me, simple theater,
have you played
my wordless play yet,

the sound of actors tramping
on the sound board of your stage?
My heart is hungry for
a splinter of that noisy wood.

It is doors that make our houses old.

THE COMET

Infants in the crib at
evening twilight we
watch our mother's luminous
eyes come near and go away.

Everything we can even think
is mythology. I mean is family.

Everything we see is our mother.
And what we see with is our father.

MONGOLIA

Once they touched
as if by accident
the smooth light they accidentally
wore as skin.

It is over now.
The bird sleeps now
and all its appetite
folds around the dry space
it wears as wings

that once over our own country
a red-shouldered hawk was
stooping from the yellow cloud
over this dusty courtyard
where small children
torment shadows with little lamps—
nightfall, the world.

THE CLIFFS AT WEST POINT

Narrow now, I count the leaves,
tules, drowned trees,
thick rusted chain against the British
stretched. Applause, polite,

the travelogue called Time is done.
A river notable for cliffs—
beautiful beside the point,
defining essence by its accidents

really, language is hilarious,
you Son of God born today
and never dying, the very words you speak
haunt the habits of the ear.

Listen. The cliffs appear.
The snow seems patchier down here.
The groove that runs our lives
a lovely mist that moves me so,

mining the soul, Storm King's
sharp drop, sky open, each
description anoints the next.
When we are the last born of the kingdom,

the cliffs appear. All questions
moot one same answer. All swans
are kinds of geese. These arms of mine
wrap tight around you, or

this body of yours constrains me
to hold tight. Unblurred,
we compress distinctness,
Irish cliffs to squeeze your river in.

THE GIANT FIGHTS BACK

A means to imbed you in my life—
So your conspiracy against my libertine
Philosophy, tense as chess, has
More than a chance of victory.

All those arches, bloodstains, white
Uneasy exudates, confetti. A dinner
With six desserts. An island
Where the few remaining whites

Scare each other every bedtime. Dread
The Indians. Dread the leprosy of sleep
That rots your daytime will.
Dream somebody, and do it. Pray for me

Who have been so meek a sinner.
Pray for my blue waves cresting
And the broken clam shells of my castle.
Pray for my lost terrors. For my sand.

THE FORMAL

for Edward Dorn

Always another
shape to locate.

For the formal is never committed
except to the sensuality of its own Researches

beseeching substance to inhabit form
or light to come down and perch upon the skin

the skin being just that nudist beach between
the sunlight's all-obliterating trombone

and your rigorous bones.

MEASURE

in memory of Louis Zukofsky

From what pontic wit, what salt in banks
       heaped high
these sheyn on-agains
       rimed
       or shivered over

       and Nausicaa, where
       is she
       whose fingers leave
       such salt in my hair?

       To allow
       a year to speak!

       then all of them!

       to let time speak as me
       never,
Second Avenue, a place
       no chicken's safe, Mother,
and once a duck.

What war was that
did we win or lose?
A dialect prov'd fatal to parole.

Agent of range, small range
of oldish autos winter nights
idling outside, a cellist humming
leaf-ferried intervals

like a deer looking both ways
and stepping across this very road,

off the staff, such hooves I said,
hoofs say you? punctum, neum, porrectus!
Lord scribble my snow.

who says,
     will this
     not serve,

     will this
     even
     not flower?

an animal
is forgiveness.

MIND THE GAP

To do it as it has always been done
is always a surprise

mind the gap

tokens and surmises
synapses, precipices.

Now the Greeks called the first condition *chaos*
or the Yawn, the Northerners said Gap
or Yawning Gap—
                          and this gap is what is

always mind, the land between—

the gap between one thought and the next.

Mind is this gap.

In our day poetry more than ever
is illuminated from that luminous domain

which it both symbolizes
and makes actual

("hears, feels")
(feeling is all)

(I speak experience)

makes actual as the live break
between the lines.

*

At the Bank station on the Holborn line, as the straight sub-
way cars come abreast of the curving platform, the voice of
a man is heard precisely and mechanically repeating:

Mind   the gap   Mind   the gap . . . . . .

warning the passengers of the six inch space between door-
sill and platform. The voice continues as long as the doors
are open.

As long as the doors are open

leap
into the gap

this ordinary mind.

Returning to the class of discussable referents
I call attention to three moderate crows
in altercation on my linden tree
—and already I bulk large in this fable

whenas my only thoughts were "crows,"
"I am protected,""there goes one
now" and "now the other two are gone."
Picture me at the window, sky empty,

tree empty. Why do I have to be at all
in this picture? You don't know me.
I'm not discussable, and you, you're
just a grammatical imputation.

But the crows were real. But whose
word are you taking that they were?
Mine? Or your own, caught by the word "crows"
into seeing black slow winds, a rainy sky?

THE WORK OF THE KILN

It is the ordinary mistake
    of the ceramicist—
flames mimic minds:
    keep this shape,

preserve this tender curve,
    hip or side
also, swelling into
    the work of walking,

keep, keep, keep. Ovens
    make the gests inside them
translucent; fire breathes
    inside the so-called object,

the clay sings, they say, hear it
    like the Bible in a bonfire
giving praise. This too (this heat-
    happy soliloquy)

is locked in a cup or a dish. Only
    your fingertips release it now
smooth whistling around the rim
    wet with a little spit.

From your mouth. Alerts me
        to a change of state:
that stanzas of long reflection
        suddenly boil—steam drives

something unperceived. A ship
carries fine china into the west. This
        is Prometheus. The sun
        sets here inside your hands

holding the glamorous smooth thing.
"Have you ever felt it, darling,
        drinking tea? You
        can feel the painted flowers,

cyclamens, I think, and primulas,
        almost in your hands."

When the cedar
waxwing lands on the barberry
branch the whole world shakes.

A BALLAD OF GOOD FRIDAY

On this day close to two
thousand years ago
the brawny Irish wrestler
Conal Cearnach

(an Ulsterman like me
but from Dunseverick)
found himself billed
for a bout in Jerusalem

with a brute from Lebanon.
Now he pondered this and that
and rested uneasy
in the curious lack of heat,

lack of sun, strange
afternoon. At first he thought
he must be getting nervous
about tonight—but that

wouldn't come till twilight,
when men eat dinner
and wrestlers fast, twisting
their silk scarves

tight in their fists,
waiting. He recognized
(being Irish and smart)
that what was bothering him

was also bothering the world—
midday darkness, thunder,
uneasiness all round, a town
getting ready for trouble.

So he walked out to the hills
and saw what we today
train ourselves to neglect:
a man dying on a stick,

and the flies were praying
round his bloody face,
buzzing their own Chaldean,
and the crowd was puzzled

that it got so little
pleasure from his dying.
The sky kept scaring them
with light and noise

then morbid silences just
when you'd expect a sound.
Conal looked around and saw
he and the dying man

were the only strangers here.
"Suppose I break your neck

and spare you pain?" he cried
in Gaelic, but the man

answered in the same and said
"Each gives what he can understand
—save your power for tonight,
I'll be finished in a minute, thanks."

Then the man cried other things
the Irishman could not recognize,
and died; Conal knew all about that,
the Last Fall, they called it,

god, the things we do to each other!
He thought about it all afternoon
while the earth bobbed and weaved
and the sun rocked around the sky.

After supper he floored his Lebanese,
walked all night and fought again
and again till he had wrestled
his old way back, still poor, to Ireland—

thought about these things for fifty years
and walked along the shores of Belfast Lough.
So many nights it's hard to sleep
with so many faces you try to understand

and a weird moon nailed up in the clouds.

SHIPWRECK

By dawn the timbers in the lowest hold were giving way—
we could hear the cantilena of the rats preparing
to move their few belongings to the upper decks,
encouraging their young to throw off fear.
All afternoon we loaded gear onto the ice
and trekked it to the nearby rocky eyot—
for so the Scotsmen called it, an island
not shown on any of our charts, not even
the Dutchman's Special or the Lybeck Hand.
The soul has powers to resist
even the nimblest music—yet we danced!
The ship was halfway down and a cheery fire
smoked away on shore. I was the last to leave—
and from the transom of my cabin door I hung
a sprig of dried marjoram for the ghosts to come
when I and all my friends had danced and sung
and written each our logbooks full
and, weary of the sport of seabirds, laid
our nibbled penholders down and died.
There is no rescue from this little world—
our chaplain shrewdly reasoned "This
is paradise, and we can call it hell
with equal justice. Whatever has no difference
is like eternity." Or so his book assured us,
where his author writes: *in the heart of a man
alone an answer argues he can never hear.*

46

It was the little thing you cared about,
the sparrow the cat had in its mouth,
that same nice muzzle we nuzzle when
it's sour sweet from yesterday's milk
and we say meow meow and it says nothing,
our bulky hands awkward under its withers,
a cat looking at us and the bird is dead.
What is the connection? Everything
is as it is, and nothing as it seems.
The sorrow of music, how it hurts the hours
we hear this piano through, years, decades even
since anything made this kind of sense.
Adieu, Abbé Liszt! And all the sense it makes
is love, the kind of love you feel
when you've finally touched each other
deeply and often enough and it's time to come
and come together if you can and go to sleep
riding out on the dark billow of wonder
that it is this one you're with and no other,
this one out of all the whole dream.

WHAT IF THE WORLD WERE ONLY WHAT IT IS AND WE STILL COULDN'T UNDERSTAND?

Disperse me. I am the nitre on your cave wall,
foxfire in your sentimental woods.
I am the lilac on your paintless fence,
the bluebeard sweetie in your backyard.
I am all the things you hoped would take
finally care of themselves, and did.
I rise in the oven, and from clouds I fall.

Strike me, I am your ruin and your kiss.
I seep into your clothes, I snore in your gullet
all night while your lovers squirm. I gamble
with all your money, you can't forget me, loathe me
all you like, I am your life. I linger
till your last minute and then I'm time.
And then I'm gone, still telling this beautiful lie.
Pour that on your ferns, this pointless ecstasy
you borrow every night, this skinny-dipping,
ants walking on your clothes, bee in your rose
trapped in your midnight. This is your only opera,
enjoy it while the audience drowses, soon
the silence after your applause will wake them
in the exhausted theater and send them home.

UNQUELL THE DAWN NOW

Then we went, high hooked from the
hardly edged dimness, dark orgulous
his high-lying soul.
Relinquish the end—out of the unexhausted roarers

rime came rilling, out of the unshopped reeds he
dares force, pale weakling—
    a weekend of mornings begins.
Under her wide womb, her fun holds to her holder,
this refreshing nun, the melodic storm-rent
beast in the cold shattered dust house,
form by guestering unfulfilled.
Nouns overawaken us, noun up staggering her
dark Sunday's feast, and worded
to the core, the game ender. So come,
day's Ward, out of ocean to us.
Undone Parnassus, fields, an underarm kiss, a heron hears
    it
o I see a day's echo wonder. Then east breaks it
on capitol, and yearlong her raven den opens.

"Come bed a fromling!" she
to us, the awaker in
the machine, building and steaming.
They faced a stoning, the silly
dark gotten roof on all the night.

War over the yowling of beasts.
Then feel us for May
and the flute and the fields and forest so wild oak,
be-sing it with canvas, the many's marrying
and eat it, with hook and sinker, this swerved
night over us stood.
Forgot like him, the stark, any dayglow slogan.

Tell me the story.
And like it, deem will fast; that,
from sweeter yogas and ages driven,
swipes restless over the barrier.
And feel it as eye gaining craft,
in the myth it hits us. When a bare
heart of her fears, spilling and lifting,
day's healing light, amid tamer cooler nostrils
the free greedy ghost comes.
Dare see leagues on earth, down a leaked acid angry one
these shiver stone and the slumberwatcher laughs!
Knock on her guest stern not! So oak weary.
                    Then mankind a loss.
This outgoing light shone for the gately gazing
                      saint intent on going.

The free endly kind, outside owns us!
Oaks are a bee's comb, and froward
the dreary laurels and oaks there holding the singers,
the sailors any answering laughter know
though I might awaken. And she wandered off
to frequent, under oaks, her birches shiny stay there.
By camp spill, for once unsaid, bar this he-rose.
Go home by doctor's loss, the ringer shout and licking
priest, the prisoner, the missing earnest kind,

50

an unaffordable lover was she and is.
And well sheathed, a bare drum tinking,
we on another thought, her frolicking on mischief,
and I'm sufficient, I'm tiger to us,
all Kore's thinking wore her tail, this cow carcass,
so old her side, her Paradise door'd
under nine paltry rocks and ten, a proof, a fated.

O as she adds time as dark hole, mutter
the folk lost for them, stalking the field
under
          (is this hearing me? is this Asia?
Two billion people always listening!
Lust of little rivers, Teesta,
is it the border? Have I forgotten?
Have I forgiven beauty for being
and not being mine?)
                    (I never tell no
nother story but under her)
                              under tumults of logic
the right thing gets said,
      on the shoulders, and all shakes all.
Tag along of bare gain, bone gone and gay worse led,
"Two versts is far standing,"
alone to reason
to God. They rue none. Over, when her
undress is too sane,
her all tan, all night said it, where?
we're naming thick, wholly unnoticed, naming
Nature! Think we, and knew, we dim baths entered?
There all is glittering born.

Sure going fast, we, the wise ones!
Woe lusts, we sons, nor any flagrant night with her.
Though younglings we, the kind hate would think,
in houses in doubt these are not friends.
She living dryfoot, even we ache
to be earnest. And she, loving dryfucked, even we eke out
the earnest sins of him easy.
And night unsounds. Ward us
in the sealed history we're given.
Night on us. All clear hours' bower, she
by the lilac tumult, then weaving these words
they shine her. Then on her unchecked screams
her chick, out of egg sooner to reek of listening.

Her golden ghosts on their side are all
oft small, when inner. Then the holy work on him
          sweeps.
Dare standing. We unwitting night to day turn.
Her ovaries fill with nectar and the ocean,
and then frolic weary after odors befell us.
Wine's in him when her adventure too sorry lives
her rude night. Beast her own, only grown worthy.
(If ever the man inside her stands
and comes out, there ends this coma.)
Drum, you greedy ones! Uncover me, Light!
To meet, I believe May, then no kissed many who're
          singing
Yes! over ending it, silly winding,
we in a saga that leaves
me there, gay song. And so each is her
mere myth, a wreathing, a blazing
when one found her gown gone, though all's a gate so.

52

MELENCOLIA

engraved for Lydia Davis, after Dürer

Be near me then, it is only a design.
Only a door painted on the wall of your room.
Go in and out. It shows a man almost naked
whose folds and shadows are prussian blue
but whose flesh where the sun strikes it
is the color of raspberries in milk
an hour after immersion. Sugar. This
is the Theologian. He is falling from heaven.
For over a week his skin has endured
the facility of his descent. The soft
bronze hairs on his forearms are burnt off.
This earth his landing place is still a sunset off.

2.
What have I sacrificed. What is the arrow
that took my eyesight, shot
from inside my cranium out, yearning
for a world it pierced me to behold.
Listen. What was the tambourine
Sally clattered as she took off her skirt
in one wide unwrapping gesture meaning me
in? At the fifteenth degree of the sign
Saturn is exalted in Libra. Buildings
are understood, measurements are known,
people understand the frustrum of a cone

by formula. The music of an immense order
peoples our love. One by one
the numbers follow him down from heaven.

3.
All that matters is this meaning?
No. He falls
and what sustains us is the detail,
pores of the skin, the map
of all our difference.
I want to tell you simply that
his body Language is who falls.
When his body touches earth we leave the room
by the spontaneously self-enchanted door.

4.
Midafternoon the heat came back.
It was a farmer with his mate,
his son with a mattock ope'd the earth
and we were two, all of us two
and never one, no one.
Midafternoon the farmer
forgot to hear his Bruckner Eighth.
All those opalescent spaces
were actual places: he moved
within them and the earth closed.

5.
This is then what Saturn sent:
the golden age, the afternoon
between the beech tree and the lilac
in the place called Europe.
The endless books of the philosophers,

the bridges of Koenigsberg.
But most a sense that our palaver
feeds and is fed by a secret stream,
a simple current underneath the mind.
That is the mind.

BLACKBERRIES

for Bruce and Cindy

These are the friends who wait for me
at the bottom of a stoneware platter
under the mound of blackberries from their yard.
Enough for a dozen they are, and
the five of us eat them all. Always
one too many (= me). Always food.
Stop eating! These are the berries
waiting under old William Powell movies
for that snide tenor voice to decide
what to blame his little woman for this time.
The garden. The dog. The rain
coming into the torn top on their shared
convertible. Things that are red.
Rhinebeck nights, old Rossiya, birch trees
sweating in the mist, a common snake
engulfing a friendly toad. The things
people talk about. The things
a heart has to hear. Here is your spoon.
There is no end to it—it is always
you, always here. Smile at them, they
feel exactly the same way about you.

HERALDRY

for Nathaniel Tarn

Slant dark top of a chain-sawed tree stump
with one white cotton glove spread on it:
Sable, a glove argent. It is a cloth

for the left hand of a woman. Or a girl, it is near
a house where some girls live, and as we walk
around it, along its walls and the walls
of its sunken garden, thing after thing,

squeezed beercans, cigarettes, a pair of white panties
also cotton, stippled with mildew yellow green,
boasting on its label One Size Fits All.

No size fits one. It is a simple system
we live in, brackish with familiar truths,

water held too long in the mouth. In the sky
snow that will fall. The flakes will sift
through the bare arbor tangled with wisteria,
will snag in the same landscape that caught gloves,
cotton, a long violent purple scarf I found

two weeks ago and set to dangle, eyesore, on a branch.
Some one came back and wore it. This glove now,
this missing hand, this emblem.

For I saw my true love's blason
cast down in colors, the dark was raining
and her hand was pale with leaving.

OF TECHNE

Now will the ironwork
of that master Isembard
Kingdom Brunel
outlast even its form,

                    that sacred

English music, the Mind—

and in its rust
revisit paradise?
This was desire
and I was hers, I left
this church
Wells, the doubled arch
to bear the double stress,
my man weight, my human longing.

Pray for all travellers. Fourth snow today
and not yet Thanksgiving. Homo
homini lupus, the river
frozen? Not yet, but last night, soft woofing,
four dogs in Rhinebeck
surrounded a coyote. They come down, they come down,
winter and its endless history. Pray
for all us travellers, never come back.
Pray that the soft woofing I hear is snow on the world
and not the hissing of the dying fire, pray
that the water boil, the lovely wife
come home through the snow,
that time remember her own
and the flame come home to the fire.

CAUSES

Trace the arrow all the way
back to its tree,
bow-string and quiver, archer
and fletcher
just incidents in its history.
One long woe
from when the tree was cut to
now. The deer falls.

CHILDWOOD

Beware the simplicity of windows
that they show a landscape you will never
by the nature of things
be permitted to enter.

It is there
and you
(whoever and wherever you are)
are here.
Language keeps you in your place.

The hills endure your absence forever.

SAMSARA

How do you like me as I am today?
Not as nice as yesterday.
The coat is grey wool and your sweater's red,
try to remember what your mother said:

Men are made of money, women lick
this honest sugar till they're sick.
This is called Society, or Home,
and it will last till kingdom come.

But the kingdom never comes and this wheel goes
and goes, the bee never wearies of the rose.

Bless me Father
For I have sinned.
Once with fire
And twice with wind.

SONGS FROM THE CHILDWOOD

1.
And if the sparrow
bothers you in the hedge
with singing with dinging
what will you do?

2.
And this woman after,
who is her little cat?
These are the arguments
that bother the begonia,
the moon can't sleep
and the dust beneath the bed moves
softly when you aren't looking.

3.
A house is made all of dying—
don't you know that?
There is no animal
but the dust is moving.

4.
Blind man, be simple,
be happy.
Your house is everywhere.

WHERE WOULD THE DUST GO
IF YOU SHOOK IT OUT

except on the very items you seek to guard.
The Chinese Chippendale with claw feet
grasping clear class balls. The dragonbacked divan,
the ormulu table from Bangkok (brought by an uncle

no one ever saw again: Uncle Siam they joked
to name him, but he was mean to your father)
and a vigorous rattlesnake plant stands tall
in the dead center of the window on the left.

Your friends tease you: You live in a funeral home,
your father is the mayor, with a house so big
you ought to be able to have a room of your own.
You don't want to. You want to be near them

on the long sloping shorelines of your sleep,
see their forms hunched in the darkness, knowing
they can see you too. Knowing they'll be there
every morning when you wake. Like the piano,

like the oak cupboard door with brass hardware
that hides the dumbwaiter shaft. You rode it once
down to the cellar you played in every day
and found it a different place that day,

silverfish quick along the whitewashed brick, the moth
fluttering over the coal in the coalbin, a life
of Napoleon fallen to the ground from somewhere,
perfectly dry and clean, you picked it up and read

two paragraphs before you knew you weren't paying
        attention,
just waiting for the shadow to move below the broken
fanlight where the hoes and rakes were kept and
        something
was moving and you couldn't read French.

THE HUNTER

I must have thought I was a kind of hunter,
the way it was when I was a kid,
you got up real early and got dressed in the cold dark
quiet as you could, treating the bedroom
as if it already was a part of the forest
and any noise could drive them away, the way
you went down to breakfast and stared at the oatmeal
as if their hoofprints streaked across it
and you could tell the way they went, the way
you set out, all of the men of you, you were
somehow a man already, and stepped quiet
over your own land to the curtain of woods,
all of you side by side but spread out, all of you
holding rifles, all of you into the woods
and before the light was full someone fired
and you fired too but you fired into the air
and nothing was killed and later you all came home
and the next time they went out you stayed home
and they had become they and you had become you,

I must have thought I was a kind of hunter
that could track you through cities and memories
and raise the rifle of simple desire against you
and make you fall down and lie there and like it
the way hunters pretend the deer must like to die
since they do it so easy and so quiet.

That a man pulls on the world
and drags it towards him
and that *towards* is the shape of all things,

the shape of things,
that if he does not pull
the blackbird comes not to the dangling
reed, if he does not pull, the butter
comes not in the churn and the shadow
does not leave the mountain—

that I have heard and heard till I'm weary
that a man is just a witness of the world
or just a member of it

whereas he is the center of it, the energy
that draws all things to himself
and by so drawing gives claws to the tiger and redness to
      the rose.

ADAM'S OFF-OX

for Mary Moore Goodlett

What is the nature of the accumulation,
the "primitive?" Man at his windowsill and
one ox passing. "Whose ox are you?"
The beat of untanned cowhide slapping
on the bony haunch—a drover's forearm.
This is my off-ox, I run him by your parlor
so you can feast your eyes—what a beauty,
hooves green with goose-shit, eyes brown as
your good wife's bush, strong as an army
and it getting paid, calm as the rowboat
tied to the lakeshore, evening, grackles
bored with the day zoom back to their island.
"Then who are you?" I am the man who owns an ox
and knows a field, and owns another
that runs wild in the red woods, a girl
not yet for milking, I am your father
and you wouldn't know me. Go back
to your soup tureen and comfortable bread,
I am the prince of destitution, first mammal,
custodian of meaningless liberties. Go sleep,
my ox already has passed your house door.
Already your little son is whimpering in his bed.

BLUEBELLS

for Tom and Jonathan

Why is the bluebell called
Endymion non-scriptus? Because
it is the one not written by John Keats.
Instead it is the one created
by Xochipilli, Lord of Flowers, or who
is the Demiurge of Vegetables, Maker
of all our green persuasion? And why
call it Endymion at all? Is it named
for pure white love
by some virgin botanizing scoutmaster,
his fingers tussling with small blue campanular flowers
while his mind is on the pale collarbones, pale smooth
paps of his loveliest lout?

THE DEMONSTRATION

What did they call it when the elephant
you imagined walking grandly and placidly
through the trees around your troubled bedroom
actually in all its blue hugeness
lofted you from your sweaty bed with his trunk
and held you in cleanness, a child in thin air,
before he laid you back gently into sleep?

What did you dream after such an elevation?
What church wall was worth your musculature
to lift powdery new cut granite hunk
by hunk into the apsidial arch you think it's called?
What did you dare to dream
more wonderful than that demonstration
of where there is to go and how many
and there you are in the world and no one sleeps?

THE BURIAL OF ROBERT SCHUMANN

Is he dead then for all the rain,
is the priest remembering his breakfast
and spooning wet earth on the noisy wood
in the gaping tenement below?

Snout of the coffin tight round him,
trumpet call, middle C closing in,
whistle and sock full of flour,
gunnysacks wrapped around your legs,

feathers in your dear hair, an indian,
raindrops pelt on elmwood of the box?
Whose hedge so drenched in April
by what church's graveyard?

Who is wood? The tin cock
on the steeple tells
his ordinary lie. The wind
will never blow again.

NURSING RESENTMENTS

Everything hurts you.
Works for your enemy, comes
like mail from the collection agency
threatening impossible punishments.
You scheme impossible retributions.

What is it for?
But what is the world for?
A father standing at the cemetery
leaning on the gate that leads to his son.

SINGING UNDER THE GROUND

I was a lad under ground, black swan among capons
and how did I hoot, and why. Who can say
why a youth youths it so wild
or turns by turns vicious or weepy,
who can say what made me leave my mother?

For I was a word in the sky, and I spoke me,
a word in the earth glowing and I wrote me
down among these dapple-witted sailors
of this most solid ocean, these brokers, these bums,
these rustling and snuffling winter not-me's.

For I was a me, and a wonder, a word without father or
     mother.

FROM THE RESTING PLACE OF THE GRAIL

The clue to unbounded transmissions from the architects
    of space
Whose least doubtless afterthought this archipelago of
    suns and
Random jests of rock whereon we live most likely is

Is (a) bronzed shoulder bared intimating braless lushness
    near to
(b) wind from ocean stirring my back hairs or the (c) man
On his way to the beach seen now again at almost
    evening,

Paenecrepuscular, postnatatory, sinucumbent mass
Market paperback perhaps read no further in than
    outward bound,
Hoarse voices of tamed beach revelers, prisoners of the
    sun.

This archipelago of frail delights. There is a final message
    (flip
Open that stolen Gideon bible to a risky passage in Hosea)
Cloaked in the sweetest merest lodging of our flesh—

That Body is innocent, and on high. That Speech when it
    listens

Says everything. That Mind that knows itself knows all.
But you, you want to know the fuselage markings on
　　　some

Turbo saucer that brought our race to this planet, you
Want to know your father's name. Be ashamed. A body is
　　　enough to have.
Stand with me on Glastonbury Tor inside St Michael's
　　　roofless tower

And look up: the patch of sky you see is your real home.
　　　I also
Fell. Suppose our heads tilted up without effort, gazing
Our way beyond the blue veil. The clue falls from your
　　　hands.

Kiss me. My mouth is the lips of your mother before you
　　　were born.

for Mary

How it felt
when we were walking
before dark,

not what I said
in my head but
how it was feeling

all round us,
the light, the infancy
of weather so strong

along the beautiful,
the river.
Looking up,

catch it
in the air
for you,

this little ball
just about to
fall behind a mountain.

2.
I am an egg. The house
is guarded by the dead.
Nobody comes

through the pale blue door
thronging and noisy.
These are the fears

I mean you to know,
saying them is funny
but you don't smile,

I feel the grit of wool
in my hands, a snail
choked on cotton thread,

a fly stuck to the sun.

THE DEATH OF TRAGEDY

HARDNESS OF THE STONE

The wooden clapper
on Good Friday
was louder than any bell ever is,

Christ the Leper
outrages us from the cross,
spoiling his body, beauty

in the kind of going
a man sees from his house door
some morning and never

steps back inside
that he should suffer
and we make music

long melisma of his dying
the vowels of *Sitio*
"I thirst" extended

from the rotten throat
to the transparent dawn
where he also stands

empty as a bell in the air.

EGGS

The connoisseur of eggs is surly at breakfast.
It is not just the Norman Conquest hair-do of the boys
(demi-punk; shorn occipitals, long locks
atop; the grease. the baggy woolly trousers).

It is the egg, itself, the very one, fetched
two days ago from the farm. Negotiations
every week the same, sometimes white, sometimes
brown as now. A very eggy egg, he thinks,

with chemicals not far. Ergosterone? Stilbesterol?
No confidence in the names of things. He sighs.
The pain is coming back, that beautiful young people
admire again, and look like killers.

There was a comet then too, a light in heaven.
How old language makes us be. Every day
he permits himself one single egg.
This one. From such precisions, which are limitations,

a music arises that can be heard in the furthest stars.
Wherever there is anyone who cares. And not even poets
think war is beautiful. His hands put down the yellow
napkin and the spoon. The general retreats from the coast.

Some other day he will see this battle through.

A FLOWER FOR THE NEW YEAR

At first I couldn't remember the name
of the vine borne flower that climbs
so scraggly up the south wall of my porch,
I see it now, bare and crazy looking, like a hank
of twine a cat got tired of bothering,
and that every spring you coax so carefully
into a few meager gorgeous deep purple blossoms,

but that we saw triumphantly tropical in the cold
rainy summer of St Barnabas Road in Cambridge,
how do they do it, the Smith's doorway and the yard
next door purple with them, visions of Persephone
and ancient excess, the wild half-unconscious
half-drunken wilful excesses of Greeks!

And then I remembered the name, clematis, and couldn't
remember if I'm supposed to say cle may tis or cle mah-
tis, like the man in the song about tomatoes
(you say, I say, let's call), anyhow, that flower,

and then I couldn't understand why I was worrying
about the names of flowers or the names of anything
or music or even the flower itself, Greeks and all
their purple antics, their raving gates and trances,
wild throats receiving and decanting seeds from
all the worlds above they meant by "Gods,"

and why should I be thinking about the gods or even
          winter
when there are men and women who have no homes
with or without flowers on the wall, men and women
who have no history except what happened to them
last night, in the street, when another man
or another woman, said, nameless, or did, motiveless,
this thing, what thing, gave, or took, or struck,
or in the common way of bleary midnight New Years
          misery
touched, just touched, and these, without a chair
or a floor to put it on, without a wall,

children only of the wind, who live in the weather
in the unromantic hate-winds of their appetite,
who suffer their own resentment more than their hunger,
whose pain is permanent, hence forgettable, always alone
but never lonely because every human being is their
          enemy
and a man fighting for his life has no time to be lonely,

and they fight, for their lives, in silence and squalor,
their stupefied eyes almost merry with glowering envy,
and I sit here baffled by the name of purple flowers,
remembering all the girls in my life as they step
naked-footed lewdly up the chill sedate corridors
of the marble museum of my heart, I worship their
          nakedness
while some man lies in the snow on Sixth Avenue with
          no shoes,

so dark the flower, shaped like a trumpet, darker
as I peek inside, or walk up down that curving bell

into the sound of what manner of sky they keep there,
who?, in the homeland of that flower whatever its name,
we do what we can and lie down in the dark, and what
          we cover
ourselves with against the wind is nobody's business,
so dark the flower, so dark the heavy traffic of names.

READING

Other peoples' eyes, their movements pass
back and forth along the lines of type
(stopping two or three times between margin and
margin) are they seeing the same words you see
and do they understand them the way you do
and put together the story of the story
to make sense to them the way it does to you?
I mean aren't you worried about the story of their
story of the story and whether it is true?
And if it is whether it's the same as you?
And what does it mean to read if you can't
even trust a collar on a shirt or a dog on a road
and all night long as you try to get some sleep
the plastic Gideon bible in the night table drawer
tells endless stories about the day of wrath
shivering the plate glass windows of motels,
noonday sinners in the hands of a jealous God?

REMEMBERING

for Joel Markman

Birds ping off the window
like some wicked game
they play in Chinatown
the end of which is soup.
Three a.m. on Bayard Street. He
is drinking Johnny Walker and I
am drinking Orange Crush.
A plate of something salty under
garlic brown shiny sauce.
Outside the steamy window
even here three dozen
years ago it's snowing.
We both are smoking
but what are we saying?
All those pale blue curlicues
that drift from his nostrils and mine,
drift on the surface of his
scotch a moment like
famous Highland mists.
I see words come out
of both our mouths
but I can't hear them.
I hear the birds of now
pursue their seeds in us.
I hear her footsteps overhead

and know I have come home
again. The terrified birds
bounce off the glass
trying to escape from the world.

ELEGY

> *for Robert Duncan dead yesterday,*
> *after sixty-nine years*

Robert when you entered the Bardo
on the west bank of the river, just
across the water from Oakland,
up Russian Hill where the round portal of the Japanese sun
opened, iris, to receive you
coming forth by day

                you saw Lama Chenrezi in His mercy
the glint of his crystal rosary
winking you towards the light, the necessary, the light,
the necessary, the light,
          the overwhelming, the light, the light,

you walked in as you used to walk into Mo's,
your eyes going everywhere at once, that greed
for information we mean by Culture, looking
for a real sleeper among the trash LPs,
wallpaper baroque and nameless performances of the
      familiar
suddenly an old Lipatti of the Waltzes, or a Petri
scuffed like shoe-leather but with the Hammerklavier
somewhere underneath the noise,
the way you walked in
glad of owning the world,
your tweed inverness

sweeping up the aisle
blessing the Messiaen and the Skalkottas you'd found,
held in the hand that held also your sacred schoolboy
          notebook
in which the Parker 51 had testified, Scribe,
to all the insinuations of this lucid day,

into the Bardo you walked and Lama Chenrezi stood
          before you
as an instance of unselfing and that pencil-point of light
that writes us away, His smile
you thought a rhapsody, you thought he was Brahms, you
          thought
his Rosary was in the hands of Dante impersonating St
          Dominic
on a chilly beach near Ravenna, where all the elderly
          infatuates
of the Law had once presided, once decided,

you saw Joachim of the Flowers, you saw our Frederick,
          saw
Ezra complaining to St Olga, saw Leopardi watch the
          sainted
bisexual moon fall like a wounded dove from heaven
into his Adriatic,
                    you thought the water lapped his feet
or else the lips of roses
nestled the worm of Love, the thorn of Karma
that ended their lives, Rilke, Scriabin,
thought it was Jack Spicer, insolent as the Stefan George
          Circle
who stood before you testing even your
dedication to the inscription of possibility

                    beyond all likelihood
                made into beauty
                        quick enough to fool
                a bumpkin's eye
                        at the state fair of the heart

you thought it was the Blessed Jesuit Robert Southwell
whose praises you made a mouth for
who stood before you, and the burning baby
was in his arms and hands, and he was not burnt

for that ardor is all kindling and never ruin,
except the ruin of our adolescent differences
that burn into the lipid flame and that
in turn into the light alone, the necessary, the light,

and you saw blazing in Chenrezi's hands, palms joined
around the glow, the fiery Jewels of Mind
in which our only refuge is, and this fire also
you took to be the heart of a man,
                                beloved, who stood
arms akimbo in the offing, lover,
waiting for you in the wicked clubs of the Gaiety
where love is served,
stretched sinews of the ordinary light, also love
speaking body speaking mind this
language stands before you
white now, white while
beyond the intelligence of chance
you yield
and into it
                the life you gave me also pour.

AN EPISODE IN LITERARY HISTORY

The Avant-Garde has moved at last so far forward that we
      can see far
off ahead of us two figures travelling in the same
      direction in which
we move. They are Homer and the poet of Gilgamesh,
      receding before
us, bright and talking. We do not seem to gain on them,
      slow as they
walk (for they are very old, this man and woman walking
      together),
but at least we finally have them in our sights.

THIS IS THE END

At any moment the sun may come out
and then be ready for it. Imagination
is the Irishman's name for whatever he wants

multiplied by whatever he lost
divided by what his mother told him to do.
Just sit there by the golden stream

like an L Street whore being cruised by limo
and let the sun find you, the water
acknowledge the pink obstacles of your feet.

Dream, buster, dream.

MONSOON

Rain. From the verandah or what
to call it, over the clumps of bamboo
I see the spires of the monastery, gilt
finials on the stupas. Sometimes
the mist gives way so that a patch of sun

touches them or leaves me grey. I have loved
all the differences in things
until I am old and they are flowering,

a crabapple stands before my northern house
murmuring suburban.
And all I have left is India.

I think of Wittgenstein,
the whereof, the thereof.
The backsliding
by which I know myself myself,

slim imputations of a far identity.
Be here. The gong goes off
over Sonada, 4:30, the dark
will be relieved from China soon,

the hill that is god
lets that one word out.

Wake. The sleep
how good it was
is over. The day

(having nothing to do with light)
begins. A book
on the shelf above your bed, snapshot
of someone you love, a candle
broken in the act of lighting,

sunshine, that long disorder,
has not come yet
but I hear it coming,
my father's footstep shuffling up the walk.

FROM A HILL IN THE BLACK FOREST

The Autobahn in Baden-Baden glistered in the summer
    sun.
Into the shade. Rest stop with blackberry pastilles and gas,
our bottle of Evian is warm. Smell asphalt here, the pines
also know their place. Noisy travellers. Is was. Was now

anticipates. A thousand miles from here cathedrals rot in
    sun
remembering Justinian and who am I? I who take you by
    the hand,
admiring your red blouse, white sailor pants, the intricate
vowels of your southernness, be mine. But who speaks?

By the end of the afternoon we were dark in hornbergs,
    firland,
stag-bellowing below-lands sudden swept green vista
    permissions
from the swerve of black road up behind the timber
    haulers.
Fall tree. Eave overhang. Water slips in the occasional
    sluice

silently remembering all the mothers that we are. The
    gravity.
The god. Here the land swept once out then back again
    one small

race of meaning something now screams down the sky.
    Hawks.
We lean on the warm car hood and think we think, and
    think we see.

BOY AMONG ROSES

for Mackay Taylor

How big is a boy, is black, wears red
singlet over white pantaloons, his feet
(its feet would be truer) are bare, his right
fist raises permanently an iron ring

that looks as if you tie horses to it
or mules. If anything is. Or scarves
to tell an absent neighbor: friends
have come and stood around his lawn

discussed his qualities and his defects,
pissed behind his elder bushes, looked
at the early-risen moon, wished he were home,
left white silk scarves, and gone. Regrets.

*

The boy is black (the word means brown,
like the strong coffee from the Farberware
left on all night (we all are drunk
on one thing or another, too many

thinks, too many hours, too many memory)
I'm drinking now with milk and sugar,

color of the stalks down there hold up the roses,
seven yards of them immensely massed

all in classic red among their own green architraves
against the iron fence, stalks or canes that lift
and disappear into the glory they propose,
humble as mothers, go on invisibly supporting

rose by rose forever we forever hope)
and wears red, and white; the red is trimmed with blue
—a little Zouave, a three-foot blackamoor
older than my father, a colored man, a boy made of
        cement.

*

His little eyes are gone, white rubble there.
Time. Or wicked boys. We look and think:
in an ecstasy of imitation this little clown
anxious to please his masters' bigotries

bugged his eyes out big like Rochester
and rolled his eyes until they rolled away.
One day. And now this other, lawnless
among roses, a boy with no eyes holds no horse.

*

Stand stiff with greeting friends
and holding horses hard against the wind.
The stallion yearneth to the mare
with all his stones, with all your main

defend him, Sammy, from his animal.
Hold a gone horse hard. Remind the wind
it has nowhere to go but to be gone.
Stare at nothing because nothing's there.

Remind the mind.

*

All neglected loves come back and scowl,
another boy stands naked in the sky.
Who are our lives? How do we answer
the woman who is gone, failed interview?

*

The way the paint is chipped, white keeps coming
        through.
The substrate (or hypokeimenon) looks grey
where the white paint's chipped, white everywhere else.
The same is not the same. We all know that

even if we know nothing else about rivers,
philosophy, the Greeks, we know nothing
and nothing is as it seems, and nothing seems
until we're there to see it, therefore

it behooves us to be gone. Dull bong
of your neighbor bell, a church is always threatening,
scaring pigeons, shooing flies that even here
want to swing and sway in this ancient sunlight

104

invading the terrace where he stands in shade,
a boy among roses he can't see or smell.
Flies can walk along his curly head
and everyone he meets could be his wife.

BONES

What makes the face interesting of course
is the skull inside it.

Without this, we look pretty much the same—
like a cupcake, brown or pink iced as may be,

left uneaten after the children's party.
Whose fanny got the donkey's tail stuck on?

Whose little whimper from the core of the heart
just won the Nobel Prize? What makes

the skeleton desirable (on the other hand)
is the cushiony seduction of the meat hung on it

by our localest demiurge, the Lady of the Womb
(with a little help from her tom).

Who is herself often the object of sedulous inquiry
by those on the prowl for delicious aggressions

such as the various hands of the body can execute
without much supervision from the brain.

Of such relationships—geometrical more than
sentimental you would think—poetry has been made

since Hector gulped Goodbye, Andromache,
and all gods' children rested among Greeks

like rare verbs in a commonplace discourse.
People do (in fact) sometimes learn from experience

and what they learn turns into the bones of their face.

AVARICE

There are children who know you. Your nose is yellow, almost golden, as you reach through the forest. What is near at hand is the small well, they call it Going to Jerusalem for reasons that will soon be clear, between the two young beeches trying to find light in the circle of six old ash trees. When the children come along, you think to yourself: Why should they enjoy their bodies all alone? I want some of that too. So you inhabit their footsteps, you move into their legs. In their shoulder muscles you make a small nest, and you throo-throo-throo like an owl in the soft afternoon. When you are tired of walking them you make them lean over the coping of the well, way over, and gaze down into the thoughtful blue faraways you have stored at the heart of the earth. You want them and they want it, the blue world down there, and up above them and you both the sad sun leans on its elbow, August, eight o'clock, the gloaming coming, where are my children now? Whose supper have they become? An impulse seizes them—but you are it, really, gold-snout—to leap into the smooth bore of the well and dwindle in blueness, wet away. They do, but it is you who push them up and pull them down, gravity is your glad gold finger, the attraction that holds earth to moon, the Moon, I should say, Eve's apple she has been trying for so many years to throw away, to hide her fault in the dark of space where no God finds anything to interest him. For thousands of years she tries but can't quite let go. It is you who holds it in her hand, you who press the word to the lip, or sink the music into the dark waxy smelly ears of old Bach at his keyboard in winter. You who take the children, wrapped in your gluttonous wings, softly down to the land below Jerusalem, below every place, the unplace, unground, where in blue they try with their last breaths to contradict your yellow appetite.

THE DEATH OF TRAGEDY

Choked with song the dictionary dies.
Awake again, thick
book of my throat, heart-bound,
dog-yeared,
             "at my age,"
        my father laughed,
"I can't tell if I'm coming or I'm going"

      the theme haunts him now, close to 90,
the little jokes he tells in dialect,
      how Rosie's husband came before he went,

the years, the temperature? degrees
                of being here,
        sacred orgasm
of the minute, of
              "the newest hour"
      Church Latin calls the end.

Awake me now, noon star, man
    of the middle,
poised ("he has poise")
    between inside-out arrivals,
                     how one woke
    and then another,
           squalling, red-haired,

preposterous all the days of my life
with prophecy, with ten lungs, with fire toothpaste
corroding my poor silences,
                         is this a life?

No, a bios, as in graphite,
not in Rome, and not a bow
to set your arrow to—
                         I am an arrow,
    kink-wood, cow-fletched—

                 he sleeps
              under Onteora only
           crow calls or thunder can
        wake him now,
eyebrows of an old house,
              a raven has bristles on its beak,
wake him
           who becomes me,
I falter for my body, lusting to find it in yours,

you reach again
           down into the furthest water.

II.

Tragedy? It is so ingrained in us now

(Igrayne sleeps, fecund, tamped full with dragon-sperm,
sleeps high in Tintagel)
so grained in us,
all that howling, all that recognizing,

we forget it is religion.
And it is ours, we absolute Greeks.

This religion: cult
of the self praised under the name of other,

as even obfusc Aristotle makes clear.

(The dear name of Jesus is my name.)

The literary history of the west turned on a millennial strug-
gle to recover tragedy, and insert it and make it flourish in
Christianity, which was and is, in its essence, a doctrine
denying tragedy. We called ourselves Christians for a while,
but the Greek religion won. Now we talk about Christ as a
name for the Self, and we are each of us Selves, Big Selves,
silent on an Attic earth, ready to suffer unredeemed and fall
into hell.

For Hell was Europe's answer, how to keep the tragedy op-
tion, favored fantasy fare for selfish men, all the sly revenges
of Euripides preserved, the mordant skepticism of Sophocles
in the face of all his failed redeemers.

Only in "final impenitence" and sacrilege could Europe find
plausible tragedy, so Hell had to be invented, and with it a
revised transcript of the old tribal god, the angry unpredictable
old man of Sinai, who smites enemy and feckless friend alike.

Only by such nonce-inventions and regressions did Europe
manage to keep its Palaeolithic religion of Big Self, Numero

112

Uno, against the transpersonal ethic of the Jewish redeemer. In his heart, every man is the Emperor. But the rabbi from Nazareth whispered: There is no emperor at all.

Buddhists have no time for tragedy. Discharge pity and terror by indulging them? An utter loss, since pity and terror would be apt materials for thought for one who would walk a certain road, good food for the journey. Not catharsis is wanted, but enlightenment. Not personal salvation, but the enlightened ability to benefit all other beings. There is no tragedy—only the infinite sadness of samsara, the infinite, endless creaking wheel of karma, only the terror of not escaping. Let this sense of me I am
be the fuel I burn
to light the way for others.

Tragedy? Only suffering, which is the raw fact of tragedy, without the glamor of consolation, the song of language. Just suffering. Our suffering and everyone's. Do not project our ignorance and catastrophes on lame Oedipus. Though all the root poisons are displayed in him, their cure is not so clearly shown. In blindness yet in certainty—yes, there is something there in the greatest of all the Greek plays, where tragedy is transumed into pious waking, and nothing is left behind for us but our own confused voices, babbling of what we saw or thought we saw among the shifting subtle breezes in the leafy suburb of Colonus. And in that mystery tragedy ended, as only Shakespeare evidently had the wit to grasp in his own golden plays so lightly called "romances"—plays where folk come to their senses before the end, and wake.

This be calling again and this be wood.
This be another man waiting for his blood.

This be tree. River already was so this
be thorn and arrogance and rice.

This be a wet cloth across my lap.
This be standing up and calling up.

Tree be tree. You be you. This be calling.
This calling be a river and be done.

Resisting the sweet sense among his legs
he came to a gentle fountain in the hill.

He prayed to it in the language of orioles
and it was silent in the language of leaves.

LINE

[Duncan McNaughton was asked in Europe why
American poets are so obsessed with the line.]

Because a line is the measure of silence
which is our science
we have embraced the ode
and chosen it over lineless discourse
by intermittency
our dance or ram
Odysseus slays to feed
ghosts into speech
is the long stream of vowelly breath cut
into meaning by the consonants just so on this round
      island
the overfluent measures of Amerisong must
cut their throats into silence.
From this is meaning
broken weather a ram or sheep is the system of the head
and ox the breath we sacrifice ourselves there is
nothing else to offer. We are the interruptions.

THE CHILD'S SONG

This little chance was all my beginnings:
There is a Lord in the Bear Skin
there is a ring he sealed around my wrist
raises my hand against this one and that one

and first against my father then my meter
then my moon. All my makers and my measurers
he made my enemies. I was little then but thick
like the lowest branches of the beech tree huge

smooth in moonlight glistering. A clearing
he found me in. This Lord he told me: Son,
no child has any father, a father
is an accident of time and water. A mother only

makes the child. You have a mother and
this complicated world. Then he locked
an iron ring around my hand and cut
a feathered arrow in my chest. These wings

he claimed will carry me beyond the world.

CARETAKERS

Our county madhouse is surrounded by lawns, well-tended, even now at the end of a very hot dry summer lushly green. The neatness is remarkable, perhaps even soothing to those who from their barred windows are free to watch the grass grow and grow, grow till the mowers come round again on their ceaseless rounds, the mowing machines grinding from first light well into the afternoon, a never-stopping howl of motors, sometimes lowering in pitch as engines idle, sometimes rising to a scream as rotors bite into the whistling stems of the fresh green, but always grinding inside the minds of the inmates who sometimes are surprised to find that the sound is coming not only from out above the cool lawns but also from inside their own chests, their own skulls, slicing through whatever may be growing, even there, in the dark.

INTO THE HUMAN LIMIT

Two old gentlemen play at their dining room table
a game of prophecy: onto the crocheted cover
one by one brightly colored cards are laid
between the decanter and the dish of walnuts
—the future so deep in love with the past!

What they see. A woman wearing schoolgirl shoes,
low heels and a simple strap snug
across her instep, fawn business suit
agreeable around the hips: pemmican for the mind
on its endless journey from never beginning
to never reaching end. Never. A sneaker, red,
in the gutter, damp. Towel squashed in the road.
Things that are wet. And this card has a
hand on it all tangled in a passing cloud.

What we hear them say:
Who comes tomorrow?
          An oafen eleve.
Who is Spartakos?
          A children slave.
And the ortolan?
          Not much but pain.
And the lovely dinner—or is it "lonely river?"
          Between the Vosges and the Moselle.
And the specialist?

In diseases you don't have.
And the foreign language?
You've read all the books in it.
And the miracle?
Easter early, milk of magnesia. Or: eat early,
memorize the meat.
And the music?
A housewife at breakfast tearing open a loaf of bread.

ON HOMER

for Linda Cassidy

It is a Jewish name, this Semite
from Lydia, Omeros, from
the root that gives in Hebrew *omer,*
"he spoke." He is the speaker,
          the stand-betweener,
as a mouth is
between the heart, that *lung,*
          and that air the ear.

He looked up from his hearing
and saw,
              a dreamy lady with meaty thighs
across from him
sat facing the light,
          memories of love and memory
of her reveries lit her smooth face calmly actual,
              light is the memory of the world,
he spoke it, saw
the cushions yielded to her settling soft

he saw, *and this is Helen*   thinks
the whole of Book III
(Gamma, the camel brings her
to the city wall, inside the silk and ramie
of her palanquin she swelters

in frangipani labyrinths of wifely anxiety—
cure my fear
by his lust,
                    cure fear by desire, cure
desire by sheer yielding, she lifts
her skirts away so a sunray falling
through her fragrant curtain fondles it

and Homer sees. Such sights as these
will blind a man in half a thousand years.

Men lift her silken litter to the roof
and she advises Priam on the names
and qualities of men,
and who knows better than she, than she
their dignities, their force
and how they wield it or withhold,
this nimble husband of hers now,
noncey, no heart in him these days for her very war,
the core, the womb of it.

She names the qualities of men and Homer hears,
and such hearing will deafen a man in a scant hundred
        years.
Then down the stone stairs goeth she
and her boudoir seeketh,
leaving the platform to the old men
whose voices, mingling, Homer likens
to the summer of cicadas, cricket cry,
a lean, sweet, practiced voicing
clear—Greeks later learned to like
their music this way, flute and timbrel, reedy clean—

122

and such singing as Homer makes them speak
will mute the lips of him who sallies it

until Homer is just a mass of feeling,
just a book.
                    Woman,
          do you know how dangerous I am,
this book of mere sensation
                    masked as a war,
     this song of mere identity
                    reckoned as hero or as god

and all it is is feeling
                         but so felt
into place the stones
of Lydia did not last longer and

the pattern of the weave
is left in the sand of the tomb floor long
after the woven cloth itself has rotted away—

this book is the pattern
of how saying
understands away
the rot of feeling,

the beautiful poison of things seen.

A crow is crying out in the emptiness of the sky
then falls suddenly away into the emptiness of the tree

It is almost twilight and a man hurries home
to the emptiness of houses, a woman
stands among the empty plates, waiting, waiting,
soon they stand among the emptiness of furniture,

empty chairs, and the mouse is scurrying
in the empty cellar, hurries till the dark comes down
onto the empty earth like a word whispered
in the emptiness of the mouth.

HORSE

Waiting at the stable for the horse to be born
the Imperial Stables
with Lipizzaners toe dancing up the parvis
delicate hooves make
small clods to rise and fall,
               the earth
           is a manner of dancing,
when will the last horse come?

The horse with the orange light in its eye,
the horse on fire, the calico horse,
the horse with the polished mirror bright aluminum rump
          mane of milkweed and dame's rocket tangled,
the horse with Latin teeth and Chinese heart,
the horse with his hoof in your lap
his wet muzzle annoying the nape of your neck wisely,
the horse with a grumbling belly the horse
with a crow on its head and a cat on its back
and the cat has blue fur, the horse of judgment,
a horse full of politics a horse full of new quarried stones
shining white in the sun, a horse
is waiting for you, his yard-long pole is
looking for you,

when will you arrive at the human destination,

when will the prefigured certainties dissolve into one
        spontaneous touch,
when will you let the last horse find you,

the horse with Roman nails stabbed into its withers,
the horse dripping with sun,
the horse whose shadow covers a dozen acres and whose
        cry
wakes you between midnight and dawn,

the horse with crazy eyes like a doting papa,
the horse with honey stuck in his throat
clearing his throat forever whence pure vowels are born
        among men,
the horse upside down, the horse stuffed with silk and
        linen and books printed in Pali,
the horse at the barricades, the green horse who stumbles
        on the wind,
the big horse who remembers your mother, the horse
who makes you love your mother, the horse
with a telephone cord garlanded round his neck,
the horse who talks to the world suddenly and in a quiet
        voice
braying the truth of the matter, the horse in orange
        leaves,
the horse with horns on its head, on grass halms grazing,
the horse on sale in New Orleans, the old horse at the
        mill, the horse
dragging the barge on the Erie canal,
the horse a slave rides all night for weeks to the North,
the horse ramping a mare in Putnam County, a horse
who will never go back, a horse with three
exiles on his back escaping into the mountains,

when will you remember your liberty,
when will you let the green horse come,
last of a thousand horses, the horse that's here even now,
        right now,
has never been elsewhere,
the horse in your cellar, the horse on your roof,
the horse in your kitchen huger than sunlight,
the horse who sleeps standing up, whose eye
stares out of your navel, the horse in your bone,
the horse with the head and hooves of a horse,
the horse running towards you on the avenue of light,
the horse that was the first thing I saw when I died?

AFTERDEATH

THE WANDERER

He broke the mind-lock and lived
however many years the earth

fantasies of the unoffended
lockstep of the sun

I tarry

* * *

I met him in Boston, his name was Harry, he was from
Maryland. He was the moon. Harry, or Ari sometimes, he said.
He was from Barcelona. "I am Ahasuerus," he said, "from
Saloniki. I am the moon."

I was patient with him week by week, in Boston it is warm,
then very cold, I waited. Finally he spoke some more.

"I am the moon. Since first I saw Him suffer on the path up
the terrible, dubious mountain of the cerebrum, outside
Jerusalem, and snickered—not meanly, *tu sais,* just nervous-
ly, nervous, since then I have been the moon. I don't know
who was the moon before. Were you?"

I was not. I was silent, though, and he went on:

"Hunchbacked or sated or hungry, trying to knife into the dark of your house too, a sickle in a window, I wander. Be safe, be a traveller, have no house. For my nervous giggle I suffer, and all of your sins too are shabby, shameful inadvertencies."

And at the end he said:

"I told a lie. If you travel, your house is the moon. Come live in me and be my will. For I am long in tarrying, and want nothing."

THE WOUNDS OF CHRIST

From the grand borders of the least concerned of all
of your daughters, kindly woman of the discrete animal
That is the broken whiffling whip you scourge your
gods with, blue-robe, competent to endow millions with
miracles
There is no other cup except this most curious gold
one your heart thought it had lost when the wind blew
But never did the sleet of dictionaries puzzle the
footsteps of augustly ceremonious if secretive Angels—
Because you were there sprinkling salt on their lumi-
nous pathways down the supple beauty of even my arm
Down the portal veins of Melanie small white cubes
on the solar plexus of Guinevere the fingers of Robert
Who hardly remembers what it was like to be
without the world around him now the battering of
inconsequential musics
Composed on the backsides of waybills, a merchant is
no one's friend, the roses of sharon jitterbug in the dune
wind
Because you are the stymied one, the preacher lady,
the forefoot down and the hind leg in hell
And I am running as fast as the equinox but your
least sarabande is quicker than this blue sheened
damascene,
My last sword, my pocket under Atlantic from which
I pluck in the damp darkness one more last language out.

Call it The Wounds of Christ that woke me from
sleep, the green bottle sleep comes in, *Vulnera Christi*

The name of our last last wine, drink this and live,
because a trifling angel fell does that keep hawks from
falling

Upward into the morning of the tree, does that keep
from my arms you lioness you godly red one you Ariel?

I press my loins to your loins and breathe the styrax
of your mane in waking over the barrier of my fingers
locked,

Mudra of I touch everything and remember it to light,
breathe me in too for I have need of your every welcome

I need your tawny gulfs your swallows I need your
insides the warm growling Aramaic of your abdomen,

Find me a way inside that does not slay us both, tree
full of pecans, tree full of almonds, tower on fire and a
hand

Shaking us both awake from dream on the last
Channel crossing I brought your papers with me to the
borderguard, This

This (I said) is my wife, this animal. The guard also
was a woman, Welcome Home! she said, meaning
England, meaning animal

She also was, every circumstance my sister, every jest
my brother, and of this mother mind we both are fleshed.

Standing at midnight
in your grandmother's house
and quietly tugging on the knobs
of the old chifferobe
till one drawer slides open and you see
in the sudden smell of powder and cotton and death
the full moon among her pale clothes
tossed back in your face from a lost mirror

SKIES

"All my life I have loved rain, especially
the corners or the edges of it, when the sky
is visible immensely, each cloud carved
into the lesser opaque hue, the Light.

All my life grey skies, grey days, carved
weather, tumult overhead, quiet differences,
wind coming and wind going, the people of the sky,
blue-black clouds, weaponstands of cumulus,

beds of brightness in the amorous air,
August over Gerritsen Beach, the clouds arriving
to tell, as we all do, more than they know.
Interpret me by looking up. All my life

I have loved that best, the intricate changeful
sky, the sky of what they call bad weather,
rain and mist and sudden openings to grey
beyond grey and white close as my mother's roof,

all my life, it fills my chest with some power
I can find no better label for than *freedom*.
This is my house. A vastness that is mine already,
a destination that seems far. It is not far.

It is telling me the size of things. My name."

136

What he meant is that the sky is permanent. It is always there. He means it is always here, and because it is, we are. It is both the sign and the situation of our continuity.

The sky is the same. What changes are the clouds.

This is the same sky that looks on the potato fields of Picardy and the dark valleys of Cumberland, it looks on Pennsylvania, and will in its season look on Mukden and Calcutta.

Since the sky is without coordinates, past and future are no different from left and right, they are pure extensions ever outing from what is no center. The sky is without coordinates, runs back in time. This sky is the one over Rouen into which the smoke of Joan's burning ascended, savor offered to the English gods. This sky will be here the day I die and you mourn me, and when you die and they mourn you. This same sky will be the first thing that Brahma sees when he wakes up again, and again makes his usual analysis, and thinks he is the first.

Same, but not the same.

Since the sky has no coordinates, men map their desires on it. These desires, once projected, take on curious names like *north* or *heaven* or *sinister,* and they become the gridwork on which further projections are densely interwoven, until you can hardly see the brightness back there.

What you see then are clouds, drifting through this vast dome the Romans called the *templum,* and divided into fours, and watched the birds move or lightning pass from one room of that great house to another, and thought by such movements

to know the world. If we see the shadow move, isn't there
a leaf, a branch, a sun, a wind?

Clouds, he is in love with clouds. Being in love with clouds
is being in love with the world.

Clouds are time, history, mystery, chemistry, love, divorce,
godheads, wheels, wars. Clouds are everything that holds us
here, rapt worshippers of what never stops happening. And
how beautiful they are, the changes.

He loves the changes, clouds, destinies, contours. He loves
the differences. He wanders in their wanderings. Cloud is
culture, the richest kingdoms have the densest clouds. And
all that beauty pours out on the bright ground, the golden
ground that never changes, the light beyond what we see when
we see light.

Then he went out for a walk and watched the pond, swollen
with two days of rain, throb over the little dam. Brown water,
its bottom mud stirred up after winter, gashed into white thick
foam, white spray in the evening light, twenty minutes or so
before dark. He is trying to explain that the richest memories
of his life, the deepest, most intensely felt personal feelings
are the most impersonal of all—light, and skies, and light hap-
pening to places. The brown light stirred and full of lastness,
lateness, quivering with impatience not to be light at all, this
brown light of the tumultuous water cresting over the old dam
wall suddenly spoke with a light he carried, locked in him,
since Christmas Eve or the eve before that in 1946 when he
walked, not cold but certainly tired, all the way home from
Fulton Street, at first under the el and then the open spaces
where Sunrise Highway starts, then the other, smaller, older

138

el on Liberty Avenue, where these city streets, smirched with scabby snow, felt clean and wonderful and *far away*—the world of such light felt, feels, far away, as if the whole sky were closer than this next iron stanchion that held the el, down which from time to time hot red sparks would gush, spurned off the tracks by the coasting iron wheels above. This brown light, cold and clean, exciting as Christmas, cold and far away, he walked through that far-away the half mile or so to his house, a child, a muffled child caught up by that light so that his own fantasies and desires were immediately, totally, but briefly, stilled, completely stilled, so that he was no one but the perceiver of light, no one but the one who walked through clean sharp iron brown light home.

WINTER MUSIC

The radiator is tired of the heat is tired of the house is tired of the weather is tired of the people who walk around in it are tired of the government is tired of listening to the voter is tired of listening to his mother is tired of her child is tired of the way we talk is tired of saying things in words are tired of the book they come from is tired of the way it is held by priests are tired of understanding the unending gloom of cathedrals are tired of standing up alone as if they were the only things on the earth is tired of the sky is tired of the sun is tired of even one more time coming again.

THE TORMENTS OF SINCERITY

a boat sideways in rapids, a telegram
floating in a rainpuddle message side up,
like a moon in a snow squall, like a man
with an eye on the clock, like a mouse
in daylight, like a priest in a hammock,
a flower in the rain, a glove on a plate,
like a street in the jungle, a book
falling from the roof, a sandwich on fire,
a river disappearing under a mountain,
like a cargo plane flying empty, like music,
like a borderguard with a heart attack,
like a subway flooded, like a window
broken by sunbeams, like an adventurer
standing in line at the airport,
like a woman in labor, like a king
suddenly doubting his ministers, like a rose
cut from its stem by an old blind woman,
like grains of sugar on the wet
lips of a sleeping child. These
are the torments of sincerity. Or is he dead?

*

What do penguins think of when they fall
deliberately bellywise off the ice cliffs

in their brief moment, a second or less,
of flying through their ancestral air
alien as Icarus, before they hit the sea?

They have hidden in the opposite element.
How can I know what the birds are thinking
when I don't even know why my voice
tightens in my chest when I see a certain woman
or what vast sky of absolute going
I long ago betrayed to flounder here

on my belly trying to soar to the light?

*

On the coldest night of the winter the sad explorers
huddle in their buffeted tent listening closely
to a cassette playing the original Paris version
of Verdi's *Don Carlos*. Their faces are close to each other
for warmth and to the recorder so they can hear
the brave determination of the tenor, the inscrutable
destiny of the Princess of Eboli, even the recorded
applause over the crazy horncalls of the mountain wind.
But long before the opera's over the men are sleeping,
the tape keeps slithering through moments of music,
and tragic lovers tryst and die and moulder
and the moon undeterred by cold climbs the sloping
staircase of the winter sky. Even the wind sleeps
but two old dead men are arguing about God.

142

A BALTIC TRAGEDY

[*The German poet Schuldt remembers as a little boy in the
last year of the Second World War seeing the beaches near
his house covered with corpses of Jewish refugees from a
rescue ship mistakenly bombed by the RAF.*]

Oelbewoelbe, a place or beach
by scant reprisal

near infarcted, as by sky the Chinese tower,
the empty. These

are the scarcities of a number
not by counting

as a tower not by seeing stands.
As.

What a surd does in the sky.
This is by the old tree

trash among shadows loved or
some things in fresh supply,

a town's name or a mother.
Redaction of a piccolo gazette.

2.
A kind of being out of focus,
example three and a half year old child in blue

on a seacoast in physiological
saline solution swims

with eyes open and sees a Wellington
sink a Red Cross boat

an enterprise of agony not adequately
impacted by "remember"

willy-nilly corpses on the shore.
Tariff quibblers lose the fresh of life,

dawn squat or hump of bread
for nothing is indifferent when you pay the price,

counting doctors to assess disease.
Numember. Turf quest

a grown man with a perfect golf
(sarsen stone, aerial metagraph).

Woke vexed into mathematics
or wear good shoes, his boarhide bluechers

muddy Bight of Helgoland. The night.
I hear the kettle sail

over the hoof tops and skirl
into the maiden windows of a skittish town

trembling for its privacy in the lord's day a.m.
A horse by watching.

The town's name sees enough.
Bloody Old king and the news of sparrows

and what is hawked in mark't, a spill
to light your history with,

good governor, postwar return of cents
to their proper musical impost

pay a carrier for his blood, a belle
for being. For a child a war

is mostly not eating. Go no further
into not knowing, The plane

was bright but the sky was brighter,
the war is never exactly over

though it's hard to find the soldiers now.
The sea was red at first

but then they cleared the mess away.

3.
This edited me he said. It edited it
was more my sense of that column

stretching from the Baltic Gate to the commissariat
where No one served Some one in a cloud,

steam table and a silver fork
cui bono for an old judge in a periwig

as my green by ground advanceth
earth upon Neaptime. The wet.

We stayed in a cheap place on the Tenison Road
not liking to pay a lot to shut the eye.

Men waiting to die still young yet
their oily bassinettes with pacifiers

jammed into the harley's shivered muffler
hurry round the corner to the other place

the one your mother wouldn't let you say
and now you can't see though you try

saturday weather but the thurs is on you
you shake your fist around the porn.

It was the town's name that eluded me
for all my root Parmenides my dog my bark

(look in this eye) each Virgilian afterthought
afternoons the lagoon. Day weather

the dry, the station's down the block, to go.
Skeptical, I married.

Terminal resonance, fast quarried
from the silences of ordinary time

specially made for your mother, carved now
by more hand than wit, a mild clavier.

I sat among Palestinians in their loud grief
mourning a century more than a country,

even the dignity of being wrong was gone them.
They are right and they lose and they lie

like the Union dead at Chickamauga.
Where am I selling? Would a man say

anything to get into bed. Noise restaurant,
parliament of cheese.

To ask you the true remaining question:
fix what would make the rest work,

any? Blood was water first
is feeble consolation, not that I asked for

or you are ladylike to give.
A color called murray and a deer across the yard.

Collar on yet, dad, with a miser waiting
and the mine weasel writhing and the bell

banging the sky apart over the methodist steeple?
Your coat on then and a white scarf

a finial? We are the only who are beautiful
with our nosegays and our final mandolins

and the girl thinking I felt your hand acrost
my whatyamacall I like it but I'll never tell

and I'll never tell by harry, cat in a window
and all the rest of us one single child

remembering a beach full of dead Jews.
I'm stuck on his remembering

burdock on my sock I can't get fast
what the cat wrote and what the dream remembered

truth finding ridiculous questions
typically rare, filling out questionnaires

confused about their original intents
(they have none, they come in cars

and wrap themselves at night in stars
like the heathen rest of us and Jesus weeps)

what do you do with what a boy remembers
inside the body of a man grown old?

That is the burden here, boat. That is the wanton,
wife. That is the kerning, friday,

that is the dog in the dump and fresh hay on the moon.
Hat for sale, will you buy me?

I read a book that told me not to count
all the numbers had a different look

and some were red and some were hooked
and some came off the page and bit me

and all the men who wrote that book
believed in ghost opinions on a vanished world

creepy as a constable in fog, his billy poised
to assassinate dissent or kick my dog.

What's your hat like? My head is in it.
Does it feel? It feels like remember

—and that's a nice girl whatever they say.
So please forget your cunning Portugals,

there are no islands here but numbers
and the numbers have no clue. The boat I meant

is gone beyond beliefs, like the color
of the orangeman and the heart of maplewood.

Uninhabited memory far sands of Thebes.
People my hat. Every word I say

sells you my hat. Whether you buy or not
is nothing but a market question. Turf

quick to yield beneath those heavy shoon,
a shandy and a capital and not just Jews

but men and women of every white
pickled pink by that sea. I'm angry now

can you read my age? Mad at the war
reminding, mad at the gaspump and the fox,

mad at the mind. Rescue
this ardent hypotenuse my remnant life,

accuse each artifice of being so
and if you do that hard

you'll find the room for me inside you
and with wet tip lip or lap

my coarse silences you of all characters imbed
in the sudden actual. My hat

is off to you, Columbus. My coat
soon follows and the smell of my chest

throws round you like a summer sky
when you woke up wanting christmas, who?

You'll find the room but the waves
will wander all the floor and men

once dead will not so easy come
sparrowfast through Edwin's living room

to illustrate the fondness of the world.
Hurry to reply. Yours, a farrier.

(A centaur even needs such handling,
ostler weather, priest on clitoris

declaiming, rites of Pan and who
dares to ride or not decide or sit

motionless while his hands caress
surgical amplitudes of your slim weather,

nay?) Some feel a tower
breaks its local sky as a boat

violates the contract of the sea
to be apart and spare all islands

from boredom by categorical philosophers
(Eve counts, Adam raises honey)

not far from where the Orinoco goes.
Serpentine though a newborn stream

an idea beginning to impose itself
local values in a fractal town

what he remembers and what the sea took down.
Call Oelbewoelbe the name of the small resort

where clouds over what the infant tells
transfer sunlight by wet mediation

through the analytical conversation
(smells like pork) onto his uncle's straw-yellow

eyelashes he will remember all his life
till he too lies in the surf and dies,

the cold clean eyes of philosophers
looking the other way. Escapist grammar

but buy my hat anyway here
give me your head to put it on.

What do you care about the numbers,
we are valves. Can it be such music

that the tower stands but the sky falls?
Hear thirty-two roads flow quickly east

a mute number of escaping slaves.

POSTCARD

In Mexico a tourist shitting in the bushes
sees a soldier with sweat-stained bandolier
find in the wiped-out rebel village
a broken mandolin and make it sound
enough of music to make both of them cry,

flow my tears he sings, *que lloran mis lagrimas*
a song he learned at puberty
one vague night studying the moon.
She watches from her awkward crouch
and hums along despite her fears

but by then the corporal has forgotten the moon.

MEN

In dreams men menstruate, get pregnant, give birth, change into water and fall into the sea, and still worse. Then the wild gibbons drenched with spray in the gorges of the Yangtze cry, and their yelling wakes men again to the ordinary world, the little tree that stands up quiet every morning.

The ram blissoms his mate
the train leaves us in the suburban
situation. The city by the lake
holds me sleepless.
In a dry country the water hides.
I want to find a word
that holds me like my breath in your hair
breathing you in and promising something
unlikely out at the same time.
The great wisdom is to find
a country where no one has to be wise.

CARTOGRAPHY

There is an area in Hungary that is mostly mountain.
Black squiggly lines close together on the wall map
so that everything looks like wombs and lips and
	sphincters
and every road is going down and the birds themselves
tremble with compassion, there are so many ways to go.

These are the muscles of somebody. Medicine bundle.
Sheaves of wheat. Someone's arm
stripped bare to its veins and nerves. And words
in the alphabet of annelids, where to say
anything at all you must leave your track in the earth.

You must. There are so many things you have to do.
This is a painting for you to mount over your narrow
	bed,
it shows the lines of things, the roads and arteries,
streams and caves and angels' neckties stretched
across the entrances to garnet caverns thronged with
	trolls.

Look up at it from your slim pillow nightly upside down.
This is the world of duty, they speak a strange language,
they wash with dust and pour air from tall green bottles

until the world is full enough for you to breathe.
Sleep then, in this garden made of one immense black
        rose.

*[This poem is for Roger Deutsch, and sketched from a
map given to me by Christina Coyle.]*

Is it the hum of you upstairs on the telephone
or bees foraging the porch's hanging plants,

a voice anyhow a kind of travelling, a purr
in the distance always making sense?

I was downstairs filling a bowl with water,
I was on the lawn talking irritably with the cat.

And is that the shower I hear now gushing
or something frying in the pan? Every element

by touching us becomes the same. Hot day.
I breathe slowly, like the entire earth.

NORMAL

Times I think there are no regular folks left in the world. Everybody's got a trick or two, and the screen door slaps closed on weird kitchens.

This beautiful young girl is old,
older than I am old as I am,
a thousand years old,

her eyes are made of blue jays
flying over roof top ice,
her skin is sunset itself
over the naked marshes

her full soft lips are red
with crushing wheat.
And don't go to sleep.

FOR COLUMBUS DAY

In between America and America is America.
They fight like hell there.
The emotions
Are only our faces
Are our fates.
What is the body of which we are the war?

Between the moon and the moon there is a shadow
This is America against America,
Our last chance against our faint hope,
A bed of gravel
Young lovers can't stop crying,
Can't touch, can't reach,

Old lovers can't stop whying, between
America and America is a war
Against the poor,
Grow wise or die, wise up and kill,
Between America and the moon
There is nothing but America,

Between the sun and the sun there is nothing
Not even a red flower
No one is hungry no one is angry
We kill and eat as a species of music
We think we are beautiful,

We kill and we eat quiet as a sheep on salt grass
Quiet as a jaguar by a waterhole,

Between a thing and a thing there is nothing,
Between a thing and a thing there is nothing at all,
That is the only difference,
That is our only hope our only hope
Let there be nothing let there be nothing
Let there be nothing between a man and a woman,
Let there be nothing between America and America.

PARTITA

Yes doctor something to follow the lines of
all the long esses of the violin
hinting outrageous puns in taffeta
rustling amidst the lower nobility
until one strokes a lady who has touched
the actual cool white fingers of the Emperor
with her white hand and heard him whisper
in her at that moment universal
feminine commodious ear
the scandalous rhyme that links earth with heaven.

STATUE OF ELVIS FOUND ON THE MOON

I saw Labrador not the Orkneys this Labrador was green
Was green from the ice the ice was around it the shore
Turned slowly into far ocean the ocean did not move
Or seem to but I had moved I was seeing I was flying
The world had come to life at the edges the lightness of
      things
Found a green hand in my hand I touched it to be to
      become

So when you talk to me about the dark I am silent
Caught in the sensual rapture of my own despair
Like David Rattray perhaps at the Reader's Digest his
      fingers
Regathering perhaps Scriabin or even Alkan
Down from the octaves of Poetic Scholarship our hardest
      book
Cutting the Arctic with a single edge the edge is green

Long before my Labrador coming over Greenland how did
      they know
The leafy minty color of winter ice from six miles up
How did Dante know the Southern Cross was visible from
      Tahiti
Was all that's left of Purgatory all that's left of Climbing
Is an ocean of air shaped like a mountain shimmering
      maybe

All that's left of Europe is a statue of Gorbachev in the
     Crimea
Scholars confuse with Jason among the Cimmerians

Gazing at the golden pelt of his wife her woolly triangle
Gathering all the glory of time into one slithering Vacancy
Maze of a maze and heart deep nestled inside the heart
Cars idle rumbling their blue exhausts like words in rain
     air
Outside the Seven Eleven radios confute the silences of
     love
Needs only a town will do it only a town is a temple
Enough from the top of it to witness the Original Star

Beaming us down from and into the curious situation of
     emptiness.

HYMN

Gods of different ages deign
To age us also through
This war of peaceful oak trees
Breakfasts of a common man

From which a genius rises
Organs refreshed and loud as April
This world-encoded empty telegram
That hints our native city's gone

The admiral lost in the winter skies
A hundred azimuths away from meaning.
Thin paper shivers in the broken light
Of unnamed sources.

WIND SWAY

Now my Diana was a naked hip, cool bedsheet,
motorcycle chrome. Now my road
was triple, my mother the next man I meet,
cricket chatter in winter wool,
dust of fire simple in old houses.

Now my Diana was a nose and not a breast
was yet uberrimous and chaste
enough, basked every morning and at twilight too
in the crystal waters of my watching.

To my south
a stream, a pond's
little waterfall.
To the north goes Cedar Hill.
West goes down the draw.

Where do I stand
to watch the operations of the mind?

The plot of land
is shaped like a bow
just beginning to be drawn

Now my Diana is an archer too
who strikes us loose
in this long childbirth of our human lives
by metaphor to wake.

Gasping in cold he stands on the bridge and sees the
          dragon move.
The star's foot on the man rests heavy.

I hear the soft tongue in her mouth, the stars, the faces
that look at us out of the dark,
insinuations of an Order I'm too dim to grasp
but bright enough to notice

but not as they are bright.
They shine as if the whole point of the night
were showing them, the whole
point of the mind to be forgetting them
into the silent practice of our lives.

AIR: FOR ENGLISH HORN

So why so
Sad the thin
Breath saying farewell to the throat
The word saying farewell to the mouth

And everything comes to that sad silent single point of
	light
The focused crystal we know nothing of but call death

And everyone comes to that and comes to it alone
Alone to that sole point of light

And goes through!
Into the healing silence
Silence in the forest silence in the meadow
After the giant falls.

Being near someone you love dying,
Is like being elected president or getting arrested
Or seeing the first glacier of the next ice age
Grinding over your little hill.
You know it happens to people all the time
        And here it's happening, and you
                Are in the happening
But it's not happening to you. Nothing
        Is happening to you.

You are nothing and no one
        To whom nothing is happening
As it happens all around you,
All around the helpless cack-handed silence that is you.

A SUIT OF CARDS

ACE
To want is my only wand.

DEUCE
Too many adventures.

TREY
A bridge remembers the future perfectly.

FOUR
Around the clock a fence to keep grass in.

FIVE
Stalwart compromises unhinge centuries of neglect
Till black men weep.

SIX
Heavy in your hand a sweater your dead love wore.

SEVEN
Room for one more the sun said rising.

OCHO
His casque of gold fall'n over hero's sweaty eyes
He condescends to die.

NUV

Broad hips of a fishing boat graze a groaning wharf.

DIX

Despair while you still can, wealthy man.

JACK

I had what I could and it took me in.

QUEEN

Bare as an inference an ivory mirror in a darkened room.

KING

Cast off!, he cried but no one listened and the shore was
        far.

POPEYE'S LAMENT

What good did it ever do me, all this strength
I littered around the world like spinach leaves
Overwhelming yuppie salads? This world is for the weak,
Who whisper and bitch and make their revolutions
Against the awful silence of their imagination
Projected outward as king or priest or president—
Their sole creative impulse is to complain.

I got the girl the girl got me, the sun
Goes in and out of the busy sea and the wind
—born from the turbine of human complaining—
Keeps everything moving and meaningless. I should
Have been a talking duck or mouse, lived
In the heroic squalor of other people's houses.

But I was me and I thought free, striving and fighting
And lifting large weights, my mouth
Always full of the wrong words, determined
To do right by my fainting beloved. And I was strong,
Strong as a book in the Bible no one reads,
Strong as pipe smoke blue in the evening sky,
Strong as a girl.

MAN

He puts his pants on his head
and walks in the town

that's what they're here for,
streets and blues

this whole world is yesterday's paper
he says and scuffs along

with his shoes in his mouth
with his wife on his back

and her wives too
and they all tell him what to do.

And when all that is Robert is gone
there still will be that which becomes Robert
        or another again and again and again
and when all of that becomer is gone
there still will be that which remembers becoming and
        staying
        and going again and again.
Only when all that is the rememberer is gone
will the simple knower stand.

RHINEBECK

Even his son is a very old man now,
the town still has trees and streets
and there the sameness ends. The mood
is other. Rich and trouble, fast, not quick.

It's like the wind: always moving,
never the same two puffs in a row,
two days. As spring comes out at last
the chimneys give up smoking,
cats uncurl like Japanese flowers
on educated lawns. Inside new glass
houses, vaguely dressed in wood and vinyl,
settlers sprinkle seasalt on their eggs

wondering vaguely as they do about everything
whether it's a healthy thing to do.

CALLING

I see your face where I have seen no one.

It is a mystery, a river, a talking dog.
Say your name. My name is noise.

She explained: he doesn't like dogs because they say his
    name,
raucous, imperator-tone, harsh calling
Robert Robert in almost one syllable.

This business of calling.

As if a prophet in a leafy elm wood
heard the sunlight talking
and the flurry of blackbirds in the leaves
made the shadows into women walking
and everything spoke.

           Most of it he couldn't hear
and most of that he couldn't understand,
but what he could, took home and made a life of,
and you believe it too, my mormons,

you who gasp to apprehend every morning in the sky
the round gold plate of the Yellow Emperor
till meaning hurts your eyes.

That you died in the winter
Means every flower
As it rises
Catches me again with your going

Carries the scrupulous
Way you had with them
To know each and each part and never general
When I barely know the names of them

But as they come, through this long cold spring,
Slowly, each one calls you to me,
Calls me to you, I don't
Know the direction, there is calling,

Coltsfoot, bloodroot—sanguinaria
We wrote love notes with the sap of,
Dharma-robe-colored, its word
From the heart—ground violet

Blue or white, periwinkle just blue,
Hyacinths, cranesbill, lily
Of the valley by the house wall in sun
Sheltering, and just today

On the roadside miles south of here
Our first warm day has brought out
Mauve and white what are they?
Takes a second or two, the names come,

Dames rocket, we liked this, we walked
Among it on our own road, pale and fragrant
Almost overwhelmed by bushes in this greenest
Spring, among the enormous memory of you.

PIGEONS

Pigeons are Jewish. They say little,
hum a lot, settle
everywhere and go aloft in minyans
searching the sky for hidden Deity.

Then strut rabbinical on lawns
contemplative, big breasted philosophers.
Reliable people! sweet
as a June breeze, lilacs

in your eyes, hazel trees, topaz
for constancy, amber for warm
slow love, remorse, desire.
Small pale messiah pecking by my side.

THE SEA TEACHES ME FRENCH

I move my tongue
inside the memory of your mouth.
Les ondes are waves, *les vagues*
are waves, *les bagues*
are gold, *de noces* are lost
au sable in my heart,
a tawny glint in sand.

Cloud wife, fade me blue.
The consummation stage:
salt-haired, you from the surf.

STUDYING HORSES

When you wake up from sleeping with women
whether or not you yourself are a woman,
there are only a few matters left to consider:
matter of the sun, matter of money,
and the matter of horses. They are grey
from sweat, whatever their color in dream
(like my cropped head of hair,
trop de parole, too many years
of talking and talking turned grey)
three matters (the way the mediaevals
—as Marlene called them—cherished
three great cycles of love:
three *matières*: of Antiquity (Helen, Ajax,
Alexander, Golden Fleece), of France
(Roland and Huon and Charlemagne),
and the Matter of Britain (Guinevere
and her tarnished, vanished cup
so many beautiful young men set out to find)
Sorry for the lecture. When you wake up
from sleeping with whatever a woman *is*
—the both of you keeping your secret,
the shared lips wet, the lap of the one
in the lap of the other—you are of course
each other's mother—you have to cope
and go on coping with directions,
the shredded manual of dream instructions

that rules the world, you woke up
clutching scraps of it, how to get there,
who to go with, who will help you,
what birds to listen to, what dragons
to leave respectfully alone,
and you lost that page, the map is gone,
you have no money and you wake up
from sleeping with women and you're gone,
it's Greenpoint again, and you took like a dope
the wrong subway to the wrong stop and suddenly
you can't remember the street of the man
—it is a man—why are you bothering
to go so far to visit a man—neither young
nor old, black nor white, why—and why
would there be a Piedras Negras St. in Brooklyn
and then you remember: it's Alvarado!
but you can't find a bus and a woman
is trying to catch a cab and she will share
—suddenly you're in a wheelchair
so she's not scared of you—without
being thrilled at the idea
but there's something wrong with her face,
and before the two of you—again, the
two of you, lost in the big world—
even spot a cab you realize
you've forgotten the number of his house,
this mystic charlatan, third world messiah
you've come so far—so far?—a subway
ride is far? where did you first
go under the ground, Egypt? o love
I am holding my own hand and praying for love—
so far to see, and all the buildings
on his block look alike—that much

you do remember—six story tenements
walk-ups with fragrant vestibules
from the dawn of civilization—
and the park of the needles—McSomething—
is not too far away. All this
is the Matter of the Sun, what we call
impoverishment: what you drag
like It over the horizon from the dark
and try to make sense of all day long,
the you and the it, inner and outer,
the drag. I know nothing about money.
And horses are grey with sweat, dry sticky,
eat sugar, wear stripes in jungles,
horses eat goats, goats catch birds,
birds swim. That much I know.
Fire flies. Water forgets. Everything
in its place. The island. Sleeping
with women. But the matter of horses
is beautiful money nowadays, verdant
sprawls of the Rhinebeck condottieri,
my cast iron circus wagon when I was five:
two heavy glossy smooth white horses pulled
a red cage with gilded wheels—and in that cart
a lion roared, I trapped it
from my other animals
—the ones with France or Austria embossed
on their pale bellies—ostrich, crocodile,
elephant, bear—and this lion,
matter of Britain, king roaring for his cup,
the grail lost behind the summer stars,
I trapped it and put it in the cage myself!
O confusion infinitely fertile we call dear world!
O spindrift credences and spontaneous theologies,

o money sloshing in the groove of time
hard, like a toilet plunger making
the blocked city be abruptly gone—
but I know nothing about that, nothing
about money, look what it did to Pound,
I would talk about horses, grey
with sea foam, sweaty with wanting,
too much time, twilights, loving someone,
les crépuscules de chevaux are the palest hours,
luminous against sumacs a white horse.

2.

When you wake up from sleeping with women
you're supposed to put money in your pocket,
get on your horse and travel into the sun-work
all the while studying other people's horses.
How they go. The colors that they have,
the arguments. In your dream you remembered nothing,
or nothing was worth it. All numbers
are wrong, think about it, wrong and count
nothing, or count for nothing. A number
is no house. Even if it was you can't find it,
can't find a street or a house or a door
and the woman with something wrong with her face
is always beside you, riding with you
into the wrong direction. They all are.
You cry some other woman's name over and over,
the one you want to be with when you're away,
awake, but sleeping with women gives you
little opportunity for being awake. Sugar
in the coffee, hair on your hair,
her name in your mouth—so much

for prepositions—the strong syllables
of her rolling in your jaws. In your dream
the grey horses were you, you pulled yourself
with painful enthusiasm from fire to fire.
Motive: take care of people. Put fires out
in tenements, look beautiful in quick streets
lathered with sexy sweat. Recite poems
into ears too easy pleased with the warm
breath of your attention. Wake. But waking
is not easy, how long your ears are
these days, fuzzy and soft, how long
your poems. The street curves up to meet the sun.
Again it is an island, one of your many
in this ancient archipelago your life.
When you were a very small boy horses still flew,
most things you ate tasted of fish, Africa
was close, clams tasted of the same
whole sea you years later would ask her
to bring you safe in her hand. It is almost noon
and your dream is a real drag, no wonder you don't
like dreaming, no wonder horses
always look so frightened, with their big eyes
rolling but their measureless will-power
keeps their scared skinny legs standing still.
A fearful thing this money is, burns,
fire in the pocket, kills birds, eats fish,
swims through the streets remembering numbers.
Money never forgets the house he lives in,
the man you still suppose yourself to want to become.
Or to want to have become already,
blue-visaged, ignorant as a mussel,
gaping, empty of alarm. Are you
even yet outside the dream,

186

are you even the one who dreamed? Trying
to find the footsteps of the morning
before you, just something to follow, you caress
the gorgeous infidelities that make you free.

WHAT

What does not show through.
What answers all questions with the identical permission.

What is not blue though some men see so.
What is listening when you aren't.
What has fewer habits than you have.
What talks about you in the mouths of others saying Joan
      is gone or John comes home.

What suffers only the constraint of its own nature—does
      it have a nature?—
What walks around in cemeteries at night with sore eyes.
What fits all the way to the bottom of the jar.
What lives alone with a cat and an eraser.

What dislikes structures and is nothing but structure.
What crossed the Pacific west to east in a hollow log.

What you see when you shake your fingers through your
      hair in sunlight and watch the dandruff flakes
      flutter away everywhere down.
What the clock on the kitchen wall is talking to.
What the dying high school geometry teacher remembers
      of first love.

MEANS

In all the Emergency Rooms
among the boxes of silk for sutures
and bubble-packs of Morpheus

consider the plastic fiasco of saline solution
clear as money
waiting on a white enamel ground

for your murky wounds.
There is always an explanation
in the sense that even in a small crowd

somebody always has a match on him.

        O love
mice eat the blind cat's food
I need you
out of the dark of ordinary longing

it is the year
year of a life

it is two years since a mountain.

in the beer garden where they did not have
the white beer that you wanted
a zither is playing,

music is metal,
no wind,

the trees have forgotten their dusty leaves,
the hair forgets the scalp

iron strings iron wings

the sky is grey with evening
o love
and I am afraid

all the old language
readies us for a departure

all day long my mother sleeps

ST SEBASTIAN SECTOR, CALVARY

On a stopped train hearing the intercom
voices discuss our local destinies
is terrible. Silence.
Until you can name it. Then
name everything. Divide it
notionally. Be rational
about where discourse rests

having risen sweet as spit in your mouth.
Bulrushes and weeds. What we sow.
Pampas grass. Mallow.

Of course her mouth was open
to help her breathe
under the oxygen mask.
No recognition, maybe once
a squeeze back to a finger squeezed.
Maybe. I said goodbye,
I kissed her forehead—
her skin just like my skin,
        her bones my bones.
Smaller. I was saying goodbye to my face.

And in her open mouth the tongue lay slack,
in the shallow dip of it something brown.
        Thickish, dried.

Food from the NG tube coughed up?
Old phlegm? It did not accumulate
in the hours I was there. Did not disperse.
She breathed, I loved her, goodbye my mother,
she died that night.

I couldn't keep the texts in mind
the funeral priest kept reciting
or the undertaker at the graveside
reading from a printed leaflet—
what do you say to the turned-up earth,
what do you say to the ground?

We mourners listen
caped against the steady rain
and understand not the least bit what it says to say.
We have to see these things
only, my sister sets
two roses down on the coffin,
we have to see.

FIN DE SIÈCLE

Being close to it again as if again
dirigibles walked along the sky
silver slug overhead a purr
of German engines *turba*
philosophorum the wise
are estranged from their book again

late roses are erased by night
and cicadas riot slow, drunks at almost dawn
croaking their more! more! more!s

Elegant forgiveness in a trice
if light is all you need.
                              I need
an Empire to rule, a house of queens
to intercede with Matter for me,
a lap to burrow in, a word to hide
deep in the flowery zenana of the dust,

I need some time to listen to what I say,
I need some time.

I need the book to come to life again and true
hear in greenwood arrows innocently thud

194

oak hunk for my pillow and a silk
ceremony before I sleep in you

immeasurable Yes.

THE PEOPLE THE FLOWERS

You walk to that corner on Avenue B
where the people have gotten together
and planted vegetables and flowers

the people the flowers

the ones who come from islands
are better at it
on this island

the people the islands

you see impatiens and think of me
upstate and pink and too old to be afraid
you see marigolds and remember all your mothers
you see dark blue pansies and recall your father
you see carrot greens leafy ferny many
and remember his music

the people the music

everything is present to you
we are all here

I entered you like an aardvark leaping in mud
I entered you like a swallow at nightfall hiding in the sky

hide in my sky

I entered you like an ice cube melting in gin and tonic
I entered you like a fly chasing a smell into a dark room

I am ugly and forever
I am beautiful and islands

the people the beautiful

the smell of the people
the whorls of everyone's hair
pores of their bodies arrayed in light
fine hairs of your nape turning clockwise or widdershins

the people the whorls

the lovely confusion of dirt and crimson zinnias
Spanish names of them
the children lick and bite each other like scientists
yearning to understand

by tongue and touch to know
the whorls of all their differences
the corner the avenues

the people the differences

the flowers you bend
you ruffle the petals of a golden chrysanthemum
your fingertips now feel

the way it feels to think of a distant city
one by the side of another bay another ocean

the people the oceans.

BY THE MILL RIVER

I sat with my mother here
the hottest day that summer
under the sycamore
and the wind came by

and the swans came by
so big and bold you said.
Now a small white wading bird,
what are you called,

white bird of distance,
on the sandbar standing?
One flies, one dies,
the water mirrors.

On the other side of the lagoon a train comes and comes.

2.
A plant of young willows
like palm trees over there on the sandy point
sea breeze on a hot day.

In this country they have a watch
tells space instead.
They have an arm

that holds you and a room
that comes to meet you
over the unspeakably
soft spring-green mosses under the shabby pines.

This room is your wedding night.
This wind is your wife.

THE ANSWER MAN

Who is my father
the man who died this morning
a bee on the high terrace of the hospital
when we were grieving

minutes before it
and before it
a smudge of new sun
cloud shabby over Oceanside

grieving at what came
at almost eight
all his chambers void his chamberlains
laid down their offices

kidney by lung by heart
his breathing slowed
the green monitor flashed
again and again its terrible question

where is the pulse
that feeds me information
I can't know anything again
who is this man?

AFTERDEATH

1.

Coming back to my place
my place coming
into a place a place
is what holds
together the breath
of it goes out and comes
in the breath of it
is always returning

2.

So I find back
to a place to find
what is mine
what is coherent
as a color is
when it is a wave
behaving a house
behaving in time
is that it a place
without interruption

3.

And mine could be a tower
held tight in air
the insertion
of one person in another
a person in a place
a summons answered
the wind came first
I have no right
to the body I am

4.

To come back to no
situation orphan house
a child is the same
something coming close to itself
I knew the shape only
of what it was to hold
bodiless the liquid place
to be alone is not the same
I am not the same as myself
only by losing that place found.

SIGNE DU MIROIR

How I have stared at that one
till the desert stretches out

and some of that glare must be my eyes
and some of that sand must be
what's left of my lust
fine grainy gritty thing blowing around

gets into your bed at night.
I have stared at my face till there is no one there.

SAMSON IN THE TEMPLE OF DAGON

Sometimes he is shown plucking the columns inward
Towards his mighty breast.
Sometimes the columns are just the right distance apart
For the heels of his hands to push them
Simultaneously outward and they fall—
Vitruvian hero poised in mortal symmetry:
He dies when the outward force exceeds the vertical
And the whole horrid house comes down on his head.

But sometimes his back is turned
Almost completely to the pillar on the left
And his arm outstretched behind him
Levers off that dark lefthand pillar
As if he were afraid to look upon
The force to which at this last hour he appeals
While his stronger hand pushes out against
The reasonable pillar of the right.

THE PERFECT STRANGER

That thing we walk around with inside, turns out to be death. Mr. Death. The question asks you—this death of yours, this Ms or Mr Death, this personage whose inner moves show in everything you do, so that even strangers can see walking in your body, keeping pace *im gleichen Schritt und Tritt,* or sitting quietly in the posture of you sitting, yourself, on the stool in the diner waiting for your eggs, this . . . What was the question? Yes, is this death, what the inner stranger turns out to be? Or is it what it turned *into,* from something else? Someone who was there before. Someone in you, all your life you felt hir stirring, you heard hem humming soft beneath your breath, or you even thought that hum was your own breathing. You felt hes fingers stretching out in yours to touch the body of somebody you love. You felt hes keenest listening curled in your cute ears (they all are). In all your ears in all your years heshe was busy listening. When young we feel the stride of this stranger inside. But now? People see who it is. Or who it has become. Or always was. The Death inside, the moonlit city, the 'lover within' and a weird grin on her faces. So that very energy that sexed him along when young, high-stepping and hard, now unveils itself as his Death, beginning his sluggish inexorable sarabande. There is only one energy. Only one. We call it lust when we're young. And what it turns into is what it is, here, the perfect stranger who rules all our lives.

AUTUMN

When the large eyes of the small
brown bear were ready to close,
they looked steadily one at a time
at each thing around him in the world
and sent it on ahead into the dark
where it would be ready for him when he slept.

IN THE HOUSE OF THE RAVEN

for Charlotte

Are the gods stronger where you are
the water thrice distilled by mountains how
we know so little of the chemistry of things
and even in the dark instead of listening
I'm always trying to make love
instead of listening to love, the fierce silence
between the molecules satin-bodiced
gold flint in the dark the cling

I'm still trying to give you an apple
no one has nibbled, a red skin no one ever saw
you told me a fresh hand could find it unprepared
perfectly strange among dark leaves
and one of us would taste it cleanly
and wonder at the quick sweet asperity
while the other's fingers felt the other's moving lips.

*

All these places were gone. The crown
or thorn. Or throne. How much
the heart won't know
of what burns or wreathes it,

what comes to settle deep inside it
speaking. How little we say
of what we know. And I
too voluble, and you too reticent,

but between us it finally gets said.

*

Eve is not far with her sad meaning
women are the targets and the victims
of rational discourse, persuasion's rape
—men invented language to trick women
women invented language to relate
compassionately to those hairy Harrys
who bear no language in their crania

inside a man's mind nothing but geometry
ballistics wordless objects ceaselessly
rearranging in a membered space
through which he stumbles with hoping hands

*

Suppose that's bittersweet growing at my window
I give it to you, things change, I know four rivers
no one wants to cross, I know too many
names, shut up Jack Donne and fold your hands
athwart your groin and sleep, it all
is architecture now, memory structures
able to cast shadows
                    suppose a rose window
glowing scarlet between one finger and the next

by flashlight color—of the northern clouds last night
when the sun and the moon were facing full
and all the churches' prayers fell back to earth
you hear them call it up and down the hall
waiting for a door to open

door to your body
but in the dark room the protectors soared
black-figured out of the wood, raven killer-whale

the wolf, a door ate you
half your body hid in the dark
outside the room

no name or taste left in the mouth
like shadows of vanished persons
suppose I could just be it, in you be simple
and you could say What is this and I could
answer I don't know taste it and see
a prayer is just a name nobody knows.

Who do I come home to be? A parable
of sun on a cold green lawn, leaves
raked and blown against the forest wall,
the little one that laps my land, this
little yard that has so many acres
all the way up to heaven light and shade
uncountable importunities of light
and nobody ever did *I got rhythm* better
than Teddy Wilson last Thruway midnight Albany.

IN TITIAN SEEN

About to put her lips
to his nipple
Venus
embraces her Adonis

capacity
of the male
to receive pleasure

not by the goddess limited
but by the fact
of patience

a man
must live a hundred years
to feel.

To feel.

*   *   *

Venus
looking at herself
older

she looks older
in the mirror

we age
by looking.
How is this

come upon me?
I hold
my face in my hand.

*   *   *

What is this black

bird white
barred chest
partridge-like

a venus bird
that walks towards the Virgin
in the San Rocco Annunciation
while the angel goes on and on
with his interminable News?

*   *   *

Bitten lips of the Magadalene
maybe time's portrait

a trick of grease
or splash of light
reminding her
how many kisses.
And now this not kiss.

*   *   *

Thirty years later
no black bird
a spill of glory
from Saint Savior's roof,
the bird comes
tumbling down
to the Virgin's
light-offering breast,
bringing light to light.
The angel herself's
astonished.

*   *   *

In The Entombment of 1560–70
one of the mourners
wears a spotted robe.
Where is God's head?
Death's tilt
hides the face of Jesus first
among the abstract

216

colors of all this sudden forgetting.
A God being put into the ground.
In that robe is Judas,
the fabric of betrayal
holding all our bodies
faithful to receive Him at the last.

Printed April 1992 in Santa Barbara & Ann
Arbor for the Black Sparrow Press by Mackintosh
Typography & Edwards Brothers Inc. Text set in
Garamond by Words Worth. Design by Barbara Martin.
This edition is published in paper wrappers;
there are 200 cloth trade copies,
125 hardcover copies are numbered & signed
by the author; & 26 lettered copies have been
handbound in boards by Earle Gray, each with
an original holograph poem by the poet.

Robert Kelly lives in upstate New York, where he has long been associated with the writing program at Bard College, and continues the practice of his own writing. Currently he's working on a *Selected Poems 1960–1990,* in the hope of helping readers find their way through his more than fifty books of poetry and fiction. He's composing three new cycles of poems: *Bliss, Espousals,* and *Red Actions,* and is finishing a fourth collection of short fiction, *The Queen of Terrors.*